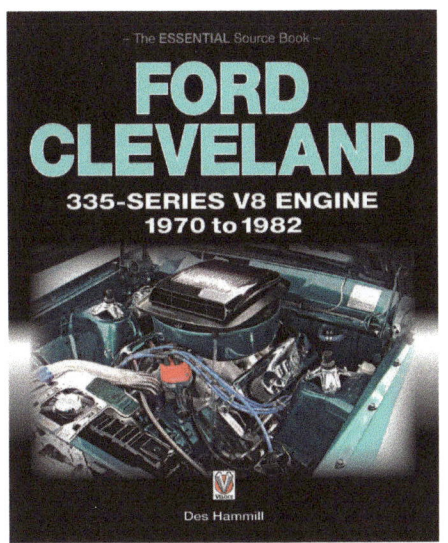

The Veloce Speedpro Series

4-Cylinder Engine Short Block High-Performance Manual – New Updated & Revised Edition (Hammill)
Alfa Romeo DOHC High-performance Manual (Kartalamakis)
Alfa Romeo V6 Engine High-performance Manual (Kartalamakis)
BMC 998cc A-series Engine, How to Power Tune (Hammill)
1275cc A-series High-performance Manual (Hammill)
Camshafts – How to Choose & Time Them For Maximum Power (Hammill)
Competition Car Datalogging Manual, The (Templeman)
Cylinder Heads, How to Build, Modify & Power Tune – Updated & Revised Edition (Burgess & Gollan)
Distributor-type Ignition Systems, How to Build & Power Tune – New 3rd Edition (Hammill)
Fast Road Car, How to Plan and Build – Revised & Updated Colour New Edition (Stapleton)
Ford SOHC 'Pinto' & Sierra Cosworth DOHC Engines, How to Power Tune – Updated & Enlarged Edition (Hammill)
Ford V8, How to Power Tune Small Block Engines (Hammill)
Harley-Davidson Evolution Engines, How to Build & Power Tune (Hammill)
Holley Carburetors, How to Build & Power Tune – Revised & Updated Edition (Hammill)
Honda Civic Type R High-Performance Manual, The (Cowland & Clifford)
Jaguar XK Engines, How to Power Tune – Revised & Updated Colour Edition (Hammill)
Land Rover Discovery, Defender & Range Rover – How to Modify Coil Sprung Models for High Performance & Off-Road Action (Hosier)
MG Midget & Austin-Healey Sprite, How to Power Tune – Enlarged & updated 4th Edition (Stapleton)
MGB 4-cylinder Engine, How to Power Tune (Burgess)
MGB V8 Power, How to Give Your – Third Colour Edition (Williams)
MGB, MGC & MGB V8, How to Improve – New 2nd Edition (Williams)
Mini Engines, How to Power Tune On a Small Budget – Colour Edition (Hammill)
Motorcycle-engined Racing Car, How to Build (Pashley)
Motorsport, Getting Started in (Collins)
Nissan GT-R High-performance Manual, The (Gorodji)
Nitrous Oxide High-performance Manual, The (Langfield)
Race & Trackday Driving Techniques (Hornsey)
Retro or classic car for high performance, How to modify your (Stapleton)
Rover V8 Engines, How to Power Tune (Hammill)
Secrets of Speed – Today's techniques for 4-stroke engine blueprinting & tuning (Swager)
Sportscar & Kitcar Suspension & Brakes, How to Build & Modify – Revised 3rd Edition (Hammill)
SU Carburettor High-performance Manual (Hammill)
Successful Low-Cost Rally Car, How to Build a (Young)
Suzuki 4x4, How to Modify For Serious Off-road Action (Richardson)
Tiger Avon Sportscar, How to Build Your Own – Updated & Revised 2nd Edition (Dudley)
TR2, 3 & TR4, How to Improve (Williams)
TR5, 250 & TR6, How to Improve (Williams)
TR7 & TR8, How to Improve (Williams)
V8 Engine, How to Build a Short Block For High Performance (Hammill)
Volkswagen Beetle Suspension, Brakes & Chassis, How to Modify For High Performance (Hale)
Volkswagen Bus Suspension, Brakes & Chassis for High Performance, How to Modify – Updated & Enlarged New Edition (Hale)
Weber DCOE, & Dellorto DHLA Carburetors, How to Build & Power Tune – 3rd Edition (Hammill)

www.veloce.co.uk

First published in 2011, reprinted 2017 and 2024 by Veloce, an imprint of David and Charles Limited. Tel +44 (0)1305 260068 / e-mail info@veloce.co.uk / web www.veloce.co.uk.
ISBN: 978-1-787110-89-2
© 2011, 2017 & 2024 Des Hammill and David and Charles. All rights reserved. With the exception of quoting brief passages for the purpose of review, no part of this publication may be recorded, or transmitted by any means, including photocopying, without the written permission of David and Charles Limited.
Throughout this book logos, model names and designations, etc, have been used for the purposes of identification, illustration and decoration. Such names are the property of the trademark holder as this is not an official publication. Readers with ideas for automotive books, or books on other transport or related hobby subjects, are invited to write to the editorial director of Veloce at the above email address. British Library Cataloguing in Publication Data – A catalogue record for this book is available from the British Library. Design and DTP by Veloce.

– The **ESSENTIAL** Source Book –

FORD CLEVELAND

335-SERIES V8 ENGINE
1970 to 1982

VELOCE
FINE AUTOMOTIVE BOOKS

Contents

Acknowledgements 6
Introduction 6

Special draughting/casting
   prefix codes 9
   ASK 9
   SK 9
   XE 9
   XH 9
   RX 9
   ZE 9
   ZX 9
   ZZ 9
Categorisation 9
Pre-1970 Ford V8 engine history .. 10
Ford engine plants 12
   North America 12
   Australia 13

**Chapter 1. Cleveland V8 engine
variants** 16
Individual model specifications ... 16
   The 335-Series 351ciM engine .. 17
   Block versions 17
   Crankshafts 17
   Crankshaft dampers 18
   Flywheels 18
   Connecting rods 18
   Pistons 18

Chapter 2. Cylinder heads 20
302ci-2V, 351ci-2V, 351ci-4V, Boss
351ci-4V, HO 351ci-4V, CJ 351ci-4V,
351Mci-2V, & 400ci-2V 20
   Valve sizes and lengths 21
   The six port and combustion chamber
   configurations: 22
   Valve split locks 22
   Multi-groove split locks ... 22
   Stock Ford single groove valves ... 23
   Valve summary 23
Stock engine valve spring
   pressures 23
   Rocker arms 24

**Chapter 3. Preparing Cleveland V8
short blocks for racing** 26
Connecting rods 26
Cleveland V8 connecting rod centre-
   to-centre distance lengths . 27
   Connecting rod-to-stroke ratios ... 29
Uprating the Cleveland oiling
   system 29
Four-bolt main cap 351ci blocks .. 31
Bore wall thickness 34
Blocks fitted with liners 34
Bore wall surface finish 35
Re-using stock-connecting rods ... 35
Connecting rod bolts 36
Blocking off the piston skirt oiling
   slots 36
Stock-connecting rods in competitive
   applications 36
Fitting four-bolt main caps onto

    two-bolt blocks 38
Oil pump drive skew gear 38

Chapter 4. Camshafts 39
Re-ground camshafts 40
Cleveland flat tappet mechanical
    racing camshafts 40
Engine oils 41

Chapter 5. Technical section 42
Torsional vibration 42
Carburettors and inlet manifolds 43

302ci engines 44
351ci engines 44
400ci engines 44
Inlet manifold options 45
Fuel 45
Engine cooling 46
    Preparation for good cooling
    capability 47
    Radiators 47
    Header tank cooling systems 47
    Water pump and alternator speeds . 47
Engine tune up 47

Parts 49
Emissions 49

**Chapter 6. Cleveland V8 racing
    history in NASCAR & Pro-Stock . . 53**
358ci NASCAR engines 1974 56
Head gaskets 56
Aluminium cylinder heads, 1982 57
Australian NASCAR blocks 57
Ford catalogue 58

Conclusion 86

Index 95

Acknowledgements & Introduction

ACKNOWLEDGEMENTS
Retired Ford USA engineers; Hank Lenox, George Stirrat, Joe Macura, Bill Barr, Wally Beaber, Lee Dykstra, Mitch Marchi, Robert Wendland, Tom H Morris and Lee Morse. Retired Ford Australia engineers; Jack Kelly (deceased), Terry O'Brian, Jim Rose, Alex Mishura, Tom Eerthardt, Ian Sheppard, Noel Wenning, Darrell Hawthorn, Alan Rose, Tony Boot, Vinko Ljubanovic, Nic Bowser, Max Lowe and Sam Stein. Ford Racing Technical; Mose Nowland and Tom Magyur. Bud Moore – Bud Moore Engineering; Ian Richardson – Wildcat Engineering; Geoff Dellow – Dellow Automotive; Simon Townley – Geelong Advertiser; Donna DeNardo – North Carolina Auto Hall of Fame; John Keane – Ford New Zealand; Adrian Ryan, Michele Cook, Brian Makin and Murray Wilson – Ford Australia; Bob Mead – Balancing Specialties, Auckland, New Zealand; Leonard Wood – Wood Brothers Racing; Lee Holman – Holman and Moody; Dave Mills, Bill Lambert, Dennis Willson, George Sheweiry, Shaun Richardson, Ray Curtis, Mick Webb, Stephen Wickham, Peter Shields, Geoff Paradise, Jan McClean, Michele Cole, Glenn Murray, Tony Devlin, Buz McKim, Dr John Craft, Rob Fischer, Red Farmer; Alex Beam of the Memory Lane Museum, Moresville, North Carolina, USA.

INTRODUCTION
The proposed enlargement of the 302ci small-block engine came about when the Ford Motor Company Truck Division asked the Engine and Foundry Division to initiate the development of a 351ci version, to fit between the current 302ci small-block, and the 390ci FE big-block engines. The Ford Division was always eager to have more powerful engines, and on hearing this information, instantly realised the potential benefits to be gained in keeping the company within the competitive market. It urged the Engine and Foundry Division to finalise the project, in readiness for the 1969 model year cars, thereby keeping them in line with those of rival companies currently manufacturing 350ci engines.

Bill Gay joined the Ford Motor Company in the Product Engine Office housed in the EEE building, after leaving Continental Aviation in the early 1950s. He had been promoted to Manager of the Commercial Engine Department by the mid-'50s, when, assisted by Tony Rocco, he oversaw the design and development of the massive V8 'Super Heavy-duty' Truck engine, produced in 401ci, 477ci, and 534ci capacities. Because of its mammoth proportions, and weighing 900lb plus, the engine became nicknamed 'Mamu' by the engineering staff. Bill Gay later became responsible for the design and development of the Ford World Tractor engine.

Bill Gay became Chief Engineer of the Engine and Foundry Division in mid-1966, having been an executive engineer since the early 1960s, and had overall responsibility for increasing the capacity of the 289ci small-block engine to 302ci, as well as the development of the 351ci Windsor small-block, and the Cleveland V8 engine. He was promoted to Staff Operations at the Rouge as an Operations Manager, in mid-1970, and, after the Engine and Foundry Division was split into two separate entities later in the 1970s, became the General Manager of the Foundry Division, a position he held until his retirement in the mid-1980s.

In mid-1966, Assistant Chief Engineer George Stirrat, who had previous experience with the design and development of the 221ci, 260ci, and 289ci small-block engines, between

ACKNOWLEDGEMENTS & INTRODUCTION

1960 and the end of 1963, was selected by Chief Engineer Bill Gay to oversee this new project, assisted by Executive Engineer Phillip Martel. George Stirrat and Phillip Martel decided the best plan of action would be to increase the stroke of the 302ci small-block by ½in, which required a block deck height increase of 1½in. To accomplish sufficient crankshaft strength, via journal overlap versus the cross sectional web area, the main bearing journal was increased to 3in, and the big-end journals to 2⁵⁄₁₆ in. They made the decision to increase the oil pump drive shaft from a ⁵⁄₁₆in to a ⅜in hexagon, to cope with the enlarged loading, and also improve the cylinder heads, by increasing the sizes of the valves and inlet ports. The overall objective was to increase the displacement of the existing 302ci small-block engine as much as possible, at minimum cost, and with maximum parts interchange. The project, starting in September 1967, took roughly nine months to complete, with the engine in production at the Windsor Engine Plant Number One (WEP1) in July 1968, ready for installation into 1969 model year cars, which were due for release October 1 1968. The engineers at WEP1 did not class it as a small-block engine, as it was too tall in the block, too wide, and had several additional drawbacks, including the 3in diameter main bearings. It did, however, fulfil the Ford and Truck Division requirements.

Following forecasts by Sales and Marketing that WEP1 would be unable to keep up with the predicted demand for these engines, a decision was made to manufacture identical engines in the USA at the Cleveland Engine Plant Number Two (CEP2), at which point it was decided to simultaneously upgrade the existing 351ciW engine to a higher specification power plant for the USA market.

Work on the 335-Series engine began early in 1968, under the supervision of Bill Gay, who, following talks with George Stirrat, asked him to select another engineer to participate in further discussions. He had no hesitation in choosing Joe Macura, an engineer he held in high regard. As was the practice at this time, because of both his expertise and high position within the company, Layout Designer Gordon Ellis automatically became involved with the project. By this stage, a directive had been issued from upper-management for the USA-made engine to have a minimum capacity of 335ci, with room for expansion, hence the title '335-Series.' However, this small sizing did not eventuate in North American production, although in 1970, the Ford Cuautitlan Plant began manufacturing a 335ci version of the 351ciW engine, specifically for the Mexican truck market.

At this early stage, during discussions between George Stirrat and Joe Macura pertaining to the cylinder head design, Joe Macura expressed his opinion that increased power would be gained by employing large canted inlet and exhaust valves. George Stirrat, for the sake of simplicity, preferred to keep the design similar to the 351ciW engine, and thought they should each design cylinder heads to their own specifications, which would enable them to compare the two finished items before making the final choice. The two resulting designs were coded 335-S and 335-M, with the 'S' denoting 'Stirrat' and the 'M' 'Macura,' and following consultation with both design engineers, the sketches for both cylinder head arrangements were prepared by Gordon Ellis and his staff.

The cylinder head arrangement designed by George Stirrat for the 335-Series was based on the current 302ci and 351ciW small-block engine cylinder head, with some minor changes, including larger valves and inlet ports to match the increased engine capacity. Stirrat firmly believed these would be the only necessary modifications to achieve a design very similar to the Canadian-manufactured version.

Joe Macura followed the canted valve route configuration, based on optimum volumetric efficiency for higher power generation, using cylinder heads not dissimilar in concept to the 385-Series 429ci and 460ci big-block engines, which Ford had introduced for 1968 model year cars.

Sales, Marketing, and Product Planning viewed both concepts, but preferred the 335-M engine, as it was considered the more innovative design, and the subsequent power it could attain would make more of an impact on the car-buying public. George Stirrat made the decision to proceed with the 335-M design, as it was, without a doubt, the preferred option of all those involved, including Bill Gay, who was most impressed with the high-performance potential. Shortly after this decision was made, both George Stirrat and Joe Macura were reassigned, and had no further involvement with the development of the 335-Series small-block engine. However, Joe Macura became manager of the Trans-Am racing programme between 1969 and 1970, when it used the 335-Series cylinder heads, which he had previously initiated, on the Boss 302ci small-block engine.

After the major decisions had been made, Bill Gay then personally oversaw the 335-Series development, constantly monitoring the progress of both the design staff and the engine through to production. During the initial design stage, he listed several ideas he deemed necessary to incorporate into any new Ford V8 engine, including making it easier to assemble. To achieve this aim, he sought to eliminate the water cross-over from the cylinder heads into the inlet manifold at the front, as this would also prevent superfluous heat entering the inlet manifold. Most Ford V8 engines used a large timing chain cover, which proved problematic to seal to the block and sump. Bill Gay was determined to address this problem on the Cleveland engine, resulting in the extension of the front portion of the block casting enclosing the timing chain, which, covered with a flat steel plate, formed the backing plate for the water pump. Although not a very lightweight arrangement, it was a pioneering idea, and solved the problem by allowing the coolant to be circulated around the cylinders, up into the cylinder heads, then down the front into the cross-over contained within the block casting. Here, the coolant from both sides of the engine mixed together, before being routed out from the engine to the top of the radiator.

Technically, the 335-Series small-block V8 engine was not an all-new design, but a development based on the existing 351ciW, aimed at producing a higher performance engine of similar capacity for the American market.

The 351ci Cleveland or 351ciC engine only remained in production in the USA from July 1969 until the end of the

THE ESSENTIAL SOURCE BOOK

351ci Cleveland block on the left, and 302ci small-block on the right: the difference between them is obvious.

1974 car model year, while the 351ciW was manufactured at the Windsor Engine Plant, in Canada, until the end of the 1996 car model year.

To remain a viable proposition, it was essential for a specified number of engines to be made per annum on an assembly line, however, as orders for the Cleveland 351ci engines decreased, the cost of production escalated, making the engine option too costly to offer, leaving Ford USA management no other choice than to phase it out. The less expensive 351ciW engines were quite adequate for their intended applications, therefore, and as the high-performance era had reached an end, it was pointless to continue the manufacture of the higher priced, heavier, and bulkier 335-Series.

In many respects, Ford engineers regarded the 351ci Cleveland engine superior to the 351ciW engine, as not only was it stronger, it had innumerable improved design features, including a 130 per cent stronger crankshaft, all blocks were four-bolt main cap capable, a simplified water pump and front cover design, better porting, larger valve area, enhanced valve cooling and improved main and connecting rod bearing proportions. The intake manifold, oil pan, and front cover sealing were all improved, and the upper block tappet area was simplified. The engine was easier to assemble in the plant, using the new two-piece rear main oil seal arrangement, compared to the rope-type, and without the awkward inlet manifold coolant transfer passageway sealing situation. The 351ci Windsor engine block deck height was 9.5in versus 9.20in for the 351ci Cleveland engine, although both had similar connecting rod centre to centre distances, and therefore connecting rod to stroke ratios.

The 385-Series canted valve big-block engine project, led by Al Martin, began in late 1964, and was to be the replacement for the existing big-block FE, made between 1958 and 1976. This engine came in 332ci, 352ci, 360ci, 361ci, 390ci, 391ci, 406ci, 410ci, 427ci, and 428ci capacities, and the MEL engines, made between 1958 and 1968, came in 383ci, 410ci, 430ci, and 462ci capacities. All these engines were eventually replaced with the 385-Series of big-block engines made in 429ci and 460ci capacities, introduced in the 1968 car model year.

Although the small-block 335-Series Cleveland and big-block 385-Series engines are very similar in their respective cylinder head designs, only the rocker arms and related components are interchangeable. Essentially, the canted valve technology descends from the 385-Series of big-block engines, which preceded the 335-Series of intermediate V8s by two years.

Design work began in late 1967, and prototypes of the 335-Series Cleveland engine were running by the end of the first quarter of 1968. They were eventually made in three capacities; 302ci, 351ci, and 400ci.

The majority of overhead pushrod

ACKNOWLEDGEMENTS & INTRODUCTION

V8 engines were problematic, as the inlet ports had to pass through the limited space between the adjacent parallel pushrods, and, therefore, they could only be a certain width. However, if the valves were canted and the pushrods splayed, the inlet ports could be significantly widened. This course of action eliminated the problem, and became the prime reason behind the eventual Cleveland engine valve arrangement.

Although by April 1968, the Cleveland engine development was progressing well, it was not yet completed, but, Ford Division asked the Engine and Foundry Division of the Ford Motor Company to provide a small-block engine, appropriate for use in Mustangs, for Trans-Am road racing. This would be used as a suitable replacement for the 1968 'Tunnel Port' 302ci engine, which had proved unsuccessful in this application. To meet this requirement, Bill Gay and the other engineers involved took the decision to fit the big port 351ci Cleveland engine cylinder heads on to the existing small-block Ford 'Tunnel Port' 302ci racing engine blocks, as for the Trans-Am circuit racing application, only the cylinder head configuration was lacking. Having been purposely designed to facilitate utilisation of the same machine tooling at the Cleveland Engine Plant, both the Cleveland and 302ci small-block engine shared identical bore spacing, at 4.380in, and cylinder head bolt placement, which made the conversion relatively simple.

Engineers modified the existing Cleveland prototype cylinder heads to achieve a different coolant flow path into the inlet manifold, to suit the 302ci small-block arrangement, and when this proved successful, they adapted Cleveland casting patterns to make what are known today as Boss 302ci engine cylinder heads. The Boss 302ci engines were in production at the Cleveland Engine Plant in July 1968, in readiness for installation into 1969 Boss 302ci Mustangs, due for release in October 1968. The Engine and Foundry Division of the Ford Motor Company produced approximately 115 racing versions of this engine, and in 1970, won the Trans-Am Championship. These racing engines varied from the stock production Boss 302ci, as various parts were stronger or of a different design, and it should not be assumed they used the same basic components.

SPECIAL DRAUGHTING/CASTING PREFIX CODES
ASK
The Advanced Engine Group, within the Electrical and Engine Engineering Department, was responsible for all new concepts for future Ford engine developments. The pre-pre-programming and tooling evaluation was also carried out in this department, after which components were alphanumerically coded with the prefix ASK. The A denotes 'Advanced' and SK 'sketch,' as engineers were able to sketch a change to any part, before making limited numbers of the item to the new specifications for further testing. The details of any modifications were subsequently entered into a book under the next available set of numbers, together with the name of the engineer responsible, which allowed other engineers easy access to any previous alterations. If, following a change, the item still proved unsatisfactory, additional modifications could be made under a new ASK code. This system allowed engineers the freedom to make experimental changes on a daily basis, without seeking permission from a higher authority.

SK
The next stage towards perfecting components took place at the Electrical and Engine Engineering Department of the Engine and Foundry Division, where the same system continued, but to different levels of development. The letter A was dropped from the prefix, which then became simply SK, although when the components were ready for mass production, they were given a regular Ford casting number.

XE
At the Electrical and Engine Engineering Department, all experimental pre-production and not fully developed components were assigned alphanumeric codes with an XE prefix. These items were not originally for mass production, however, some may have been intended for Original Equipment/OE production release. Although many were, XE coded components were not always necessarily for racing engines. The Ford XE-192540 NASCAR block was considered experimental and not a production part, although there was a possibility of this in the future. Quantities of individual items, including blocks, were made with an XE casting, which never went into mass production.

XH
When all race engine activities were transferred to Special Vehicle Engine Engineering at Car Product Development in early 1970, the code prefix became XH, and applied specifically to this department.

RX
Signifying 'Race Experimental,' the RX prefix was given to all build-up assembly and build requirements for racing engines; there could be several versions within this code. As an example, in 1969 the RX-452 Cleveland race engine builds were assigned this code, and retained it until 1970. There were two series of engine builds, with each separate series titled Series I or Series II. RX would not be seen on the actual components, only the build sheet – the components could be drawn from many sources at Ford.

ZE
Mustang production part.

ZX
Mustang racing component for 'Off Highway Use Only' carrying no warranty.

ZZ
Mustang performance and service part.

CATEGORISATION
As Ford new registration vehicles became available from October 1, it is always necessary to think in terms of car model years and NOT calendar years when categorising Ford cars.

As an example, the 1963 car model year production stopped at the end of July 1963. New car model year update body and trim alterations were incorporated into the assembly lines throughout the following month of August, with production of the new 1964 car model year vehicles beginning early September, and subsequently shipped to the dealerships in late September, ready for sale on 1 October 1963.

The mid-year introduction of the 1965 model year Mustang became

THE ESSENTIAL SOURCE BOOK

available in April 1964, which was a strategic move on behalf of Ford, in order to offer a new car to the public, when no rival company was doing the same, and in doing so, produced much media interest, in turn proving very beneficial to the sales figures. In 'Ford speak,' there is not, as is often stated by the press, a 1964½ model year Mustang. However, from 1 October 1964, a few simple updates were added for the 1965 car model year, giving the appearance of a new model; a situation that has caused considerable confusion amongst enthusiasts over the years.

PRE-1970 FORD V8 ENGINE HISTORY

The side-valve Ford V8, introduced in 1932, was 221ci with a 3¹⁄₁₆in bore and 3¾in stroke. The three main bearing crankshafts used Babbitt bearings, from 1932 through to the 1936 model year, but, from then on, shell insert bearings were employed. However, in 1938, these engines changed from 21 to 24 studs, and in 1939, the capacity was also increased to 239ci, by way of a bore increase to 3³⁄₁₆in. Ford and Mercury cars used both engines until 1941, when America entered WWII.

A scaled-down version of the original side-valve engine, to become known as the V8-60, with a capacity of 136ci via a 2.600in bore and a 3.200in stroke, was introduced in 1938, and, although originally designed specifically for the UK market to suit the vehicle tax laws, was also used in the USA until 1942. This engine was not favoured by American consumers, as it was insufficiently powerful for heavy cars, but became highly popular in oval track Midget Racing applications. Simca acquired this engine and produced it in France in its original 136ci/2227cc capacity during the 1950s and 1960s, and, between 1957 and 1963, in 143ci/2351cc form via a 3¾in stroke crankshaft. The engine was last produced in Brazil.

Although the 221ci was phased out at the end of the WWII, 239ci engine production was resumed. The capacity was increased to 255ci by means of a 4in stroke crankshaft in 1948, and both this engine and the 239ci remained in production until the end of the 1953 model year. A larger capacity 337ci engine, weighing in the vicinity of 530-570lb, with a 3½in bore by a 4⅜in stroke crankshaft, was made and introduced for 1948-1951 model year Ford trucks, and 1949-1951 Lincoln cars.

Specifically for Lincoln-Mercury, in early 1948, Ford upper management took the decision to change the V8 engine from side to overhead valves, and, within only a few months, the design for this project was in progress. The 317ci EAD Lincoln V8 was first introduced in 1952 model year Lincoln cars, and, the same year, the 279ci EAL version became available in Ford light trucks, heralding the overhead valve Ford V8 engine era; the 317ci EAD engine had a 3.800in bore by a 3½in stroke, while the 279ci EAL was 3⁹⁄₁₆in bore by a 3½in stroke. At this time, all Ford engines were allotted three-letter identification codes, until the introduction of the FE in the mid-1950s.

The 317ci EAD engine was installed in 1952, 1953, and 1954 Lincoln model year cars, before being increased to 341ci EAM for 1955 and 1956 cars, via a 3.937in bore and a 3½in stroke, and finally to 368ci ECU for 1957, with a 4in bore and a 3.660in stroke.

The Lincoln V8 engine was also used from 1952 through to the end of the 1955 model year in 279ci EAL form in Ford trucks, as was the 317ci EAM 1954 and 1955. It was used from 1956, in 302ci form with a 3⅝in bore by a 3.660in stroke, and as a 332ci with a 3.800in bore by 3.660in stroke, through to the end of the 1964 model year in 700, 750, and 800 Ford trucks. Both forms had forged crankshafts and gear drives to the camshaft; that is, two gears with a reverse rotation-configured camshaft, and were always known at Ford by their capacity, as opposed to a three-letter code.

Prior to manufacture at the Dearborn Engine Plant, the Lincoln V8 engine was developed in the Engine and Electrical Engineering building in the Lincoln-Mercury Department at the Ford Research and Engineering Centre in Dearborn, under the overall direction of senior engineer Victor Raviola, with second-in-charge chief designer and department manager Paul Clayton managing the programme. Roughly 1.4 million Lincoln car and Ford truck overhead valve V8 engines of this type were made between 1952 and 1964, when production ceased.

During WWII, long-serving Ford engineer, Victor Raviola, was involved in the overall development of the Ford V12 aircraft engine, but on completion, the US military informed Ford it was no longer required. Instead, it needed a large capacity V8 engine, suitable for powering tanks. To supply this demand, Raviola removed four cylinders from the original aircraft engine, resulting in the GAA 60-degree 500bhp V8 engine. As it retained all the basic aircraft specifications and construction methods, it was a fairly sophisticated and efficient tank engine.

A decision was reached to build an additional overhead valve V8 engine, more suited to the smaller, lighter Ford cars, needing less engine torque than the extremely heavy Lincoln cars. Design work for this began towards the end of 1950, under the management of the same team responsible for the Lincoln V8, resulting in the Ford V8, a slightly smaller and lighter derivative of the original that was being manufactured at the new Cleveland Engine Plant Number One.

The design features of the Lincoln overhead valve V8 engine included a cylinder bore spacing of 4.630in, employing four-bolt retention per bore or ten bolts per cylinder head, with the cylinder head inlet ports siamesed, 'ram's horn' style exhaust manifolds and a 'deep skirt' cylinder block, which was a carry over from the side-valve V8 engine era.

At Ford, these engines were always identified as the Lincoln V8, and not the Lincoln Y-block V8. The individual versions were identified by the three-letter codes EAD, EAL, EAM, EBJ, and ECU, although the automotive press and enthusiasts have retrospectively named them Lincoln Y-blocks. Subsequent Ford Y-block engines became known at Ford as Y-block V8 engines.

The 239ci EBU Y-block Ford V8 engine was introduced in the 1954 car model year in Ford cars, and also in 256ci EBY form in Mercury cars of that year. The 239ci Ford engine had a 3½in bore by a 3.100in stroke, while the Mercury 256ci engine used a 3.620in bore, and for 1955, the engine capacity was increased to 272ci and 292ci. The 272ci

ACKNOWLEDGEMENTS & INTRODUCTION

ECG maintained the Mercury bore size at 3.620in, but the stroke was increased to 3.300in, while the 292ci ECH engine had a larger 3¾in bore. The 272ci engine was fitted into Ford 1955-1958 model year cars, with the 292ci used in cars through to 1962, and, until 1964, was installed in trucks. The 312ci ECZ version introduced in the 1955 Thunderbird sports car had a 3.800in bore by a 3.440in stroke. The 1957 model Thunderbird was the last to use this engine, but it saw service until 1960 in Mercury cars. Although the Ford Y-block was lighter than the Lincoln V8, as it weighed approximately 650lb, it could by no means be classed as lightweight.

Initially, Ford Y-block engines were made at the Cleveland Engine Plant on one assembly line, until a second was added a few years later, but in 1961, one line was stopped and converted to make the 221ci small-block Fairlane engine. When Ford Y-block production was halted in 1964, an approximate total of 2.9 million had been made. Then the tooling was eventually sent to Ford of Brazil, where manufacture of these engines, to power both cars and trucks, began in the late 1960s, and continued until the mid-1980s.

In 1954, design work began on the Ford Engine (FE) big-block V8, as it was deemed necessary to build larger capacity engines to go beyond the capabilities of the Ford Y-block, allowing them unique engines within the car model ranges. Production of both 332ci and 352ci versions was in progress at the Dearborn Engine Plant by mid-1957, ready for introduction in the 1958 new model year cars. The 332ci engine had a 4in bore and a 3.300in stroke, and was used between 1958 and 1959, while the 352ci with a 4in bore by a 3½in stroke was used between 1958 and 1966. This was followed by the 361ci engine as used in the Edsel in 1958 and 1959, which had a 4.047in bore by a 3½in stroke. The FE engine for the 1961 car model year was 390ci, with a 4.050in bore by 3.784in stroke, and was last produced in 1976. This was followed in late 1961 by the 406ci High-Performance FE, with a 4.130in bore by 3.780in stroke, and 385bhp in four-barrel Holley carburettor form or 405bhp with triple two-barrel Holley carburettors. For 1963, the 427ci High-Performance FE, with a 4.233in bore by 3.870in stroke, was offered with single four-barrel Holley carburettors, with 410bhp, or in two four-barrel Holley carburettor form with 425bhp. 1965 saw the single overhead camshaft/SOHC 427ci FE become available, with 615 and 657bhp. Ford introduced a 410ci and 428ci FE for 1966, with a 4.050in and 4.130in bore respectively, both using a 3.980in stroke crankshaft. The 410ci engine was for 1966-1967 Mercury cars only. A 360ci short stroke version of the basic 390ci engine was produced for 1968 truck applications. On average, these FE engines weighed 730-750lb, depending on the cylinder heads and added accessories, the last being used in passenger cars in 1976, and in trucks in 1978.

As a means of increasing capacity, the original Lincoln V8 was replaced by the Mercury, Edsel, Lincoln/MEL engine, in 383ci, 410ci, and 430ci capacities, for the 1958 car model year. The 383ci had a 4.300in bore by a 3.300in stroke, and was available between 1958 and 1960. The 410ci, a 4.200in bore by a 3.700in stroke, was presented for 1958 only, and the 430ci engine, a 4.300in bore by a 3.700in stroke, was offered between 1958 and 1965. The 383ci engine powered Lincoln and Mercury cars, while the 410ci was used only in the Edsel, whereas the 430ci engine was used in Thunderbirds and Lincolns. The largest capacity this engine series attained was 462ci between 1966 and 1967, for use in Lincoln cars. On average, the MEL engines, made at the Lima Engine Plant in Ohio, weighed 740lb, or a little more, depending on accessories.

As product planning and sales marketing had advocated the necessity of differentiating between Ford and Lincoln engines, extra capacity was not therefore the sole reason for developing these two new big-block V8 engines in such quick succession.

Ford introduced its massive 'Super-Duty' gasoline engine in the 1957 production model year for trucks in 401ci ECL, 477ci ECM, and 534ci ECN capacities, and this series lasted until 1982. The 401ci engine had a 4⅛in bore and a 3¾in stroke, the 477ci a 4½in bore by a 3¾in stroke, and the 534ci a 4½in bore by a 4.200in stroke.

During the mid-'50s, Ford amalgamated all the various sections within the Product Engineering Office of the Engine and Foundry Division. From this time, rather than Lincoln-Mercury, the Truck/Commercial and Ford Engine Engineering departments were working separately and being accountable for their own projects – just one overall management structure became responsible for all the engines designed and developed throughout the Ford Motor Company in North America. In Ford-speak, this re-structuring exercise became known as 'Commonisation.' Following this adjustment, the management structure was altered, and Engine Engineering, for example, comprised of the chief engineer, followed by two or three executive engineers, department managers and section supervisors, principle engineers, design/product engineers, mechanics, and detail draughtsmen. During this management reshuffle, Paul Clayton became an executive engineer and Robert Stevenson, who had been a section supervisor, became chief engineer of Engine Engineering, followed by Bill Innes in mid-1959, Emmet Horton mid-1965, Bill Gay mid-1966, and George Stirrat (who, in mid-1966, had become the first assistant chief engineer) in mid-1970.

The Ford Motor Company had a unique hierarchical management system headed by the president, followed by vice presidents responsible for a range of divisions. There was, for example, a vice president in charge of the Powertrains Division, where all engines, gearboxes, and rear axles were made, overseeing a range of general managers within that division. The Engine and Foundry Division was a sector of Powertrains and was comprised of four parts; the Product Engineering Office, all the engine manufacturing plants, all the foundries, and the Controllers Office. The Product Engineering Office had responsibility for the Lincoln-Mercury, Truck/Commercial, and Ford had its own body, chassis, engine, and transmission engineering departments, but following 'Commonisation,' one body, chassis, engine, and transmission department served all three.

The company also used a grading system for salaries in engine engineering, with the top level of this scale pertinent

THE ESSENTIAL SOURCE BOOK

to the skills of the recipient, with no bearing on the length of service. The Vice President of Powertrains would have been graded at 24 or 25, the general manager 21, chief engineer 18, assistant chief engineer 16, executive engineer 15, department manager 13, manager with no design responsibility 12, section supervisor 11, principal engineer 10, senior design engineer 9, design engineers/product engineers 8, administrative non-engineers 6 or 7, mechanics/build up/dynamometer operator 4 or 5, detail draughtsmen 3 or 4, and secretary 2 or 3.

Promotion within this company was based on aptitude and not length of service, as eligible candidates were invited by management to be considered for a higher position, and at no time did personnel apply for the vacancy. Each selected member of staff was given an assignment, which, on completion, was subsequently assessed by a superior engineer based on all objectives, including keeping within the allotted time-frame, meeting the given budget, and obviously the quality of the finished item. There were four grades available; firstly 'Excellent/Outstanding,' only awarded for a perfect execution of the task, then secondly 'Satisfactory Plus,' for work regarded as very acceptable. The third level 'Satisfactory' signified that although the task had been completed, the person concerned had limited ability, and finally 'Satisfactory Minus,' which meant complete lack of managerial qualities. Recipients of this grade effectively stood no chance of future promotion.

The 221ci small-block Fairlane V8 engines, with a 3½in bore and a 2.870in stroke, went into production in July 1961 for installation into 1962 model year cars. However, later in the same year, it was enlarged to 260ci via an increase in the bore to 3.800in, which was further increased to 4in, making the 289ci version for the 1963 car model year. The 221ci engine was phased out in mid-1963, and the 260ci at the end of the 1964 car model year. For the 1968 car model year, the 289ci engine stroke was increased to 3in, to make a 302ci engine, and the 289ci was phased out just before the end of the 1968 production year. Ford always referred to the 221ci, 260ci, 289ci, and 302ci small-block engines as the Fairlane V8. The Boss 302ci small-block engine was introduced for the 1969 car model year, remaining in manufacture until the end of the 1970 car model year. The 351ci Windsor small-block engine, a development of the small-block Fairlane V8, went into production in Canada at WEP1, for fitting into 1969 model year cars. The 351ciW engine remained in production until the end of the 1996 car model year at WEP1, but manufacture of the 302ci/5.0l small-block Fairlane V8 continued until December 2000 at CEP. On average, the small-block engines weighed 430-460lb, but the Boss 302ci and the 351ciW were approximately 500 and 510lb respectively, with the 335-Cleveland engine, which was a further development of the 351ciW engine, weighing in the region of 550lb.

The 385-Series 429ci and 460ci big-block engines were introduced for the 1968 car model year and continued in use until 1998, while the 370ci truck version introduced in 1978 only ran through until 1991. The 370ci truck engines had a 4.050in bore by a 3.590in stroke, the 429ci a 4.360in bore by a 3.590in stroke, while the 460ci had a 4.360in bore by a 3.850in stroke. The 385-Series engines weighing an average 650lb eventually replaced the MEL and FE big-block engines.

Between 1952 and 1970, Ford USA introduced eight different families of gasoline/petrol passenger car and truck engines, and between 1952 and 1980, within this range, made 41 different capacities, and roughly double that number of individual engine versions, using two, four, triple, twin, and twin four-barrel carburettors, special cylinder heads, and various heavy-duty parts in combination.

The Lincoln V8, Super Duty, FE V8 engines were all made at the Dearborn Engine Plant, the Ford Y-block V8, the 221ci, 260ci, 289ci, 302ci, and Boss 302ci small-blocks and the 335-Series 351ci low-deck engines in the Cleveland Engine Plants, and the MEL and 385-Series at the Lima Engine Plant; all these plants were situated within the USA. The Windsor Engine Plants in Canada made 289ci, 302ci, 351ciW, and the 351ciM, and 400ci 335-Series engines, the Cuautitlan Engine Plant in Mexico produced 260ci, 289ci, 302ci, 335ciW, and 351ciW engines, and the Geelong Engine Plant in Australia manufactured 302ci and 351ci low-deck 335-Series Cleveland engines.

FORD ENGINE PLANTS
North America

Cleveland engines were eventually produced at three Ford engine plants. In the USA, production began in July 1969 at the Cleveland Engine Plant Number 2 (CEP2), finishing in 1974. Ford USA made the H-code 351ci-2V (1970-1974) and M-code 351ci-4V (1970-1971), the R-code Boss 351ci-4V in 1971, the Q-code Cobra Jet (CJ) 351ci-4V-CJ (1971-1974), and the R-code High Output (HO) 351ci-4V (1972-1974). A reported 3,711,700 Cleveland engines were made here between mid-1969 and mid-1974.

The M-code 300bhp 351ci-4V engines were used in the De Tomaso Pantera cars between 1971 and 1974.

The 351ci engines manufactured in the USA between 1969 and 1974 were equipped with either a two- or four-venturi carburettor, and to differentiate between the two, were listed as 351ci-2V or 351ci-4V, with V signifying venturi; 2V indicated the lowest, and 4V the highest powered version of the engine.

The first two Cleveland engines were the 351ci-2V and the 351ci-4V for 1970 model year cars, and both employed the same two-bolt main cap blocks, but different cylinder heads, inlet manifolds and carburettors. The 2V engines had 'open' combustion chambers, small inlet and exhaust valves and ports, and a two-barrel carburettor and inlet manifold, while the 4V engines had 'closed' combustion chambers, big inlets and exhaust valves, a four-barrel carburettor and inlet manifold. The 351ci-4V engine cylinder heads are highly favoured over the 2V for racing applications.

In 1971, Ford introduced a 400ci Cleveland engine, which was made in the Canadian Windsor Engine Plant Number 2 (WEP2). When the USA-made 351ci-2V Cleveland engine was being phased out in 1974, the Windsor Engine Plant Number 2 began production of the 351ciM engine. A reported 990,000 of the 10.3in tall deck Cleveland engines were produced between 1971 and 1981.

ACKNOWLEDGEMENTS & INTRODUCTION

The first Cleveland V8 engine produced at Geelong was tested on November 12, 1971. Key Ford Australian Engine Engineering staff left-to-right are: Erin Duniam, Russ Rawson, Jack Hawke, Norman Dalton, Neville Wight, and Jack Kelly.

Australia

Ford Australia imported approximately 6000 289ci-2V and 289ci-4V small-block V8s from Ford USA, for fitting into 1967 XR Falcons, and roughly 11,000 302ci-2V and 302ci-4V engines, for 1968 XT Falcons.

Initially, the XW GT Falcon, introduced in mid-1969, used the 290bhp 351ciW-4V engine imported from Canada, and the Phase I GTHO used the same basic engine equipped with a 600CFM Holley carburettor, a Ford Muscle parts hydraulic camshaft, with all other engine parts remaining as per standard. Ford Australia imported in the region of 17,000 302ci and 351ciW V8 engines from North America throughout 1969, however, the 351ciW V8 was phased out in 1970 and replaced by the 351ciC V8. From August 1970, the XW GT Falcon used the new 300bhp 351ciC-4V engine imported from the USA, while the GTHO Phase II used the same basic engine equipped with a 750CFM Holley carburettor, as opposed to a 600CFM, Ford Muscle parts mechanical camshaft, and a dual point distributor. In 1971, the number of V8 engines imported increased to 23,000, and, of this total, roughly 4000 were 300bhp 351ci-4V Cleveland V8 engines for their later XW GTHO and all XY GTHO Falcon cars, the first of which was available around April 1970. The remainder were 302ci-2V small-block and 351ci-2V Cleveland V8 engines for installation into Ford's Falcon, Fairlane, and LTD cars of the same era.

The late 1971-1972 XY GT Falcon used the 300bhp 351ciC-4V engine as imported from the USA, and the GTHO Phase III engine was fitted with a 780CFM Holley carburettor, twin point distributor, a mechanical camshaft, and tubular exhaust manifolds.

In November 1971, Ford Australia began manufacturing 302ci-2V and

THE ESSENTIAL SOURCE BOOK

351ci-2V Cleveland engines at the Geelong Engine Plant, ready for installation into XA Falcons in March 1972, but it was a little later before it began producing 351ci-4V engines. At this time, all components were made in Australia apart from the blocks, which were imported fully machined from the Cleveland Engine Plant USA.

The Ford Foundry, formerly named Ensight, stood on North Shore Road, Geelong, which had previously housed the British company Birmid Auto Castings. A workforce of between 1400 and 1500 was employed at the plant, working two shifts a day, five days a week, and, in order to fulfil orders, when necessary, an additional shift was possible. V8 cylinder heads were cast in pairs and the plant could process 100 boxes an hour, equating to 200 items. Cylinder blocks and cylinder heads were cast using Ford's AC plain cast iron with main caps, and flywheels cast in ACB, as per standard Ford practice. Using the shell moulding process, this plant could produce nodular iron 302ciC and 351ciC crankshafts at the rate of 120 per hour.

As soon as Ford Australia received notification of the imminent halt in 351ci Cleveland engine production at the Cleveland Engine Plant in 1973, an order was placed for roughly 60,000 machined blocks, to tide it over until it was able to produce its own at Geelong. The tooling up process began in 1973, with all necessary production equipment expected to arrive in Australia during 1975. While blocks were being cast in mid-1975, they could not be machined at the Geelong Engine Plant until early 1976 because of the damage incurred to the five machines supplied by Buhr Machine Tool Co during transit to Australia in late 1974. During a hurricane, a bulldozer in the hold of the ship broke loose, seriously damaging the cargo, which necessitated the machine tools being returned to Buhr in the USA, where, due to the extensive damage, they were rebuilt before being re-shipped. Many of the original components were re-used, but only those guaranteed to be in perfect condition. Consequently, the machine tools had to be re-qualified, but as the Cleveland Casting Plant (CCP) had stopped production of the relevant blocks, none were available, and, to allow this process to go ahead, Ford Australia air-freighted around 30 of its own raw blocks to America

During the re-qualifying process Buhr found that, unlike when previously used on the USA blocks, the life expectancy of the cutting tools for boring the cylinders, camshaft, and main bearing tunnel bores was not being reached, so a block was sent to the Cleveland Engine Plant for a metallurgical check. Here, it was discovered that, although it fell within Ford specifications, the Australian Pig Iron had superior wear resistance properties. However, Buhr overcame this problem with a change to higher specification tungsten carbide cutting tooling.

When, in 1975, the Geelong Foundry began making its own cylinder blocks, they were made during day shifts with smaller less complex components than at night. Using a 10-ton capacity Cupola, the plant had the capability of casting 90 Cleveland V8 blocks an hour, or roughly 750 per day, over an eight or nine-hour period. It required 240-250lb of cast iron to actually pour one of these blocks because of the risers and runners, even though the finished machined article only weighed between 170 and 172lb.

The USA-made blocks have CP casting markings, while the Australian blocks from 1975 are marked GF with appropriate day and date casting codes, indicating when they were poured.

Ford Australia chose to make the Cleveland engine, as not only was it the newest design of small-block Ford V8, but also one block could be common to two engines, and was therefore a better option than the 302ci and 351ciW small-block engines.

Importation of 351ciW engines from Canada ceased in late 1969, and the 302ci small-block V8 from the USA early in 1971.

The 351ci-4V engines manufactured in Australia for XA Falcons from 1972 onward were essentially a 351ci-2V fitted with a four-barrel carburettor, but with open combustion chamber cylinder heads, and not the closed variety of the earlier USA-made engines. They also did not meet the performance level of the American counterpart.

The Geelong Cleveland V8 engines were used in XB Falcons from October 1973 until June 1976, XC Falcons July 1976 to March 1979, XD Falcons March 1979 to March 1982, and finally in XE Falcons from March 1982 to November 1982. The ZF, ZG, ZH, and ZJ Fairlane, FA and FB LTD also used these engines between March 1972 and November 1982.

Best estimates, over the entire production run from November 1971-December 1981, are: approximately 210,000 302ci and 351ci Cleveland V8 engines were made, with no more than 10 per cent being 302ci. In general, the car-buying public preferred the increased power attainable from the 351ci over the 302ci, which was considered an economy V8 engine.

On average, the Geelong Engine Plant could make between 70 and 120 Cleveland V8 engines per day, and throughout this ten-year period was in production for around 220 days a year. More engines were made per year between 1972 and 1977 than at any other time, with the annual total number slowly diminishing as the years went by, until Ford management decided to cease production in the early 1980s, at which point, the daily production number was reduced to just seventy.

Originally when Ford Australia took the decision to gear up to make Cleveland V8 engines, as opposed to importing them fully built, it had expected to be producing 150 per day, and more with extra shifts. However, the anticipated demand for V8s failed to materialise because of the first oil shock and subsequent fuel crisis in the early 1970s, which saw a considerable reduction in demand for these engines. However, this fall in production was not the primary reason for the cessation of its manufacture in this country, as this was mainly due to an upper-management decision that the V8 had run its course, and that in its view, six-cylinder engines could adequately equal the performance qualities they provided for a road-going car. Although on the basis of engine efficiency this was true, a number of the Ford car-buying public still sought V8 engine-powered cars, and in an effort to regain its customers from GM, it re-introduced the 302ci/5.0l small-block engine.

Between November 1971 and 29 April 1976, when the first Australian-

ACKNOWLEDGEMENTS & INTRODUCTION

made block was used, Ford Australia imported approximately 90,000 Cleveland V8 engine blocks. Between May 1976 and the termination of production in December 1981, it also made and machined around 120,000 engines, including 'build ahead stocks' of approximately 10,000 blocks and assembled engines. Throughout 1980, Ford Australia shipped approximately 150 Geelong 351ci Cleveland engines to Ford USA, intended for service replacements.

The last Cleveland V8-powered car off the assembly line at the Geelong Plant was a Falcon, on 25 November 1982.

During the late 1960s, Completely Knocked Down (CKD) Falcon and Fairlane cars were exported from Australia to Ford of South Africa, where they were subsequently assembled at the Ford Port Elizabeth Plant. Apart from slight differences, the South African XY Fairmont GT cars were essentially Australian specification XY Falcon GTs. The 1973 fuel crisis saw the cessation of V8-powered cars, but until this point in time, Australia also supplied Ford of South Africa with CDK Fairlane cars, to be powered by 302ci-2V and 351ci-4V Cleveland engines.

Perfectly restored 1973 Australian-built XA Falcon 351GT as photographed in 2009 at the Queensland Raceway, near Brisbane, Australia.

Chapter 1
Cleveland V8 engine variants

As there was both a low-deck block, with a centre of the crankshaft axis to the top of each block deck size of 9.206in/232.8mm, and a tall-deck height block, with a centre of the crankshaft axis to the top of each block deck size of 10.297in/261.5mm, various components were necessary therefore, and so there were several differences within the range of Ford V8 335-Series engines.

The USA-made 351ci-2V and 351ci-4V, and the Australian-made 302ci, 351ci-2V, and 351ci-4V engines all used the low-deck blocks, while the Canadian-produced 351ciM and 400ci versions used the tall-deck block.

As two different main bearing sizes were employed, the 335-Series engines used two types of crankshaft, with the low-deck blocks using those with small, 2.750in/69.9mm diameter main bearing journals, while those used in the tall-deck blocks were larger, with a diameter of 3.000in/76.3mm. The Canadian-made 351ciM and 400ci Cleveland engines employed blocks with 3.000in/76.3mm diameter main bearing journal crankshafts, and all other engines used the smaller components, with a 2.750in/69.9mm diameter.

The 335-Series engines employed three different stroke lengths, with the 302ci using a 3in, the 351ci a 3½in, and the 400ci a 4in.

INDIVIDUAL MODEL SPECIFICATIONS

The USA-made 351ci-2V and 351ci-4V engines had a 4.000in/101.6mm bore by a 3.500in/88.90mm stroke crankshaft, with small 2.750in/69.9mm main bearing journal diameters in a 9.206in/232.8mm low-deck block, together with a two-bolt main cap block.

The Australian-made 302ci stock production engine had a 4in/101.6mm diameter bore by a 3.000in/76.20mm stroke crankshaft, with small, 2.750in/69.9mm main bearing journal diameters in a 9.206in/232.8mm low-deck, with a two-bolt main cap block.

The Australian-made 351ci-2V stock production engine had a 4.000in/101.6mm diameter bore by a 3.500in/88.90mm stroke crankshaft, with small, 2.750in/69.9mm main bearing journal diameters in a 9.206in/232.8mm 'low-deck' two-bolt main cap block.

The Canadian-made 351ciM engine had a 4.000in/101.6mm bore by a 3.500in/88.90mm stroke crankshaft, with large 3.000in/76.3mm main bearing journal diameters, in a 10.297in/261.5mm tall-deck, and a two-bolt main cap block.

The Canadian-made 400ci engine had a 4.000in/101.60mm bore by a 4.000in/101.6mm stroke crankshaft, with large main 3.000in/76.3mm main bearing journal diameters in a 10.297in/261.5mm tall-deck two-bolt main cap block.

The 1971 USA-made Boss 351ci, the 1971-1974 Cobra Jet 351ci-4V, and the High Output 351ci-4V engines of 1972-1974 all had four bolts on the centre three main caps.

The Australian-made 351ci-4V engine had a 4.000in/101.6mm diameter bore by a 3.500in/88.90mm stroke crankshaft, with small 2.750in/69.9mm main bearing journal diameters in a 9.206in/232.8mm low-deck, with two-bolt main cap blocks.

In later years, when some Australian-made 302ci-2V and 351ci 2-V engines were stripped down for repair or rebuild, they were found to be fitted with four-bolt main caps on the centre three main bearings, as opposed to the expected two-bolt components. These very rare blocks are amongst the 300 returned from the 1981 SVO 366 NASCAR order, which were fitted into

CLEVELAND V8 ENGINE VARIANTS

Australian crankshafts are easily recognised by their 302 and 351 numbers on the casting. ARD1AE 6303 appears on both castings. A stands for 'design source Australia,' R for 'righthand drive,' D for the year code, 1 for the car model year, A for 'engine size and special features,' E for transmission, 6303 means crankshaft and A or B after the numbers for first or second design revision respectively.

production engines before the end of 1982, in order to put them to use.

The 335-Series 351ciM engine

There were two distinct versions of the 351ci Cleveland engine, a situation that evolved when the USA-made 351ci was phased out, and Ford Canada began manufacturing a 351ci alongside the existing 400ci engines at WEP2 for 1975 model year trucks. Although Ford made a new 3½in stroke crankshaft and different pistons, both WEP2 engines used the tall-deck 400ci engine block, connecting rods, cylinder heads, and inlet manifold, together with other common components, to create this second model of the 351ci engine. Based on cost effectiveness, the aim was to produce the second model 351ci using as many existing 400ci engine parts as possible.

To differentiate between the two versions of the 351ci Cleveland engine, the letter M, (for 'Modified') was placed at the end of the code, and although made for 1975-1979 model year cars and trucks, it was 1982 before the entire stock of engines was finally utilised.

Block versions
1. USA 351ci low-deck two-bolt main cap stock production block.
2. USA Boss, HO and CJ 351ci low-deck four-bolt main cap stock production block.
3. Canadian 351ciM and 400ci tall-deck two-bolt main cap stock production block.
4. Australian-made 302ci and 351ci low-deck two-bolt main cap stock production block.

All stock production blocks were essentially cast alike, with no difference in wall thickness between two- or four-bolt main cap blocks, as the variation between them was confined to the different main caps. The registers of both two- and four-bolt blocks are identical as machined into the block, which means that four-bolt main caps can be fitted to any two-bolt main cap block, have two extra holes drilled and tapped per main cap, and the block with its 'new' main caps fitted then align-honed.

It should be noted that, although at first it may seem feasible, it is not simply a case of bolting a set of four-bolt main caps on to a two-bolt block, in the expectation that the additional caps will line up with the existing main bearing tunnel bores as machined in the block. In the first instance, the four-bolt main caps have to be checked for fit in the block registers, which means they must be a 'snap in fit' and not merely positioned by hand. The main caps are longer than the register into which they fit by 0.0005-0.0007in/0.0127-0.0177mm.

A main cap that fits loosely into a block is of no use whatsoever, and any attempt to use one in this condition often results in 'spun main bearings.' The main caps MUST fit tightly into the block's registers, and the main bearing tunnel bores re-sized to stock factory dimension, which, in the case of low-deck blocks, is 2.9417-2.9425in/74.719-74.739mm. All engine reconditioners are very familiar with this procedure, with many having specialised align-boring or align-honing equipment to perform the task.

Crankshafts

All base model Cleveland engines had cast iron crankshafts at the stock Ford mix of a nominal 30/40 per cent nodularity. Irrespective of this, all crankshafts made met Ford's durability requirements, and, apart from the odd case, there was no failure rate. The 1971 Boss 351ci and the HO 351ci engines of 1972-1974, on the other hand, were both fitted with crankshafts made exclusively from 90 per cent nodular iron or maximum-nodularity iron, and checked to verify they met the specification. The 90 per cent nodular iron crankshafts had substantially more tensile strength than the stock components.

The stock production nodular iron 351ci crankshafts do not break when turned to 7000rpm, if fitted with lightweight aftermarket connecting rods and forged pistons

The nodular iron used by Ford is also known as 'ductile iron' or Spheroidal Graphite iron/SG iron, and is grey cast iron impregnated with nickel, magnesium or cerium bearing alloys during its molten state at Ford's Speciality Foundry, Dearborn. Plain cast iron was used wherever possible on the basis of cost. However, there were instances when components,

THE ESSENTIAL SOURCE BOOK

including main caps, some crankshafts, and crankshaft dampers for heavy-duty applications, needed additional tensile strength. To meet this requirement, Ford used three basic grades of nodular iron. Throughout the 1960s and 1970s, 90 per cent/100 per cent nodular iron was used in the manufacture of components such as flywheels for high-performance engines, which were tested for 'no burst' to 12,000rpm. 80 per cent nodular iron was used for high-performance engine crankshafts and main caps, while the stock Ford production engine cast crankshafts were made from approximately 30/40 per cent nodular iron and not tested for nodularity after manufacture; there is little difference between 90 and 100 per cent nodular iron.

Crankshaft dampers

The stock production engine crankshaft dampers were made from grey cast iron, while the 1971 Boss 351ci and the 1972-1974 HO 351ci engines had crankshaft damper hubs and rings made with 90 per cent nodular iron. Schwitzer Inc and Simpson Industries both supplied Ford with crankshaft dampers, but in the case of the High-performance Cleveland engines, they were made by the latter. The 90 per cent listing by Simpson signifies maximum possible nodular content. The 1971 Boss 351ci and the 1972-1974 HO 351ci crankshaft dampers are the ideal components for high rpm operation over any other stock items. These engines were fitted with higher-than-standard rated inertia dampers, tuned to respond to the torsional vibration they generated. The hub and ring were made using nodular iron, as opposed to grey cast iron because of its higher tensile strength, and the resistance to breakage it afforded. The elastomer was bonded to the hub and damper ring, in an effort to prevent any permanent location change of the ring to hub, under extreme operating conditions that could cause it to lose its designated position in relation to the hub.

Flywheels

The stock Cleveland engine flywheels were plain cast iron, but 90/100 per cent nodular iron was used to make those of the 1971 Boss 351ci, and the 1972-1974 HO 351ci engines and tested as 'burst proof' at 12,000rpm for 2 minutes. The maximum recommended rpm for a stock cast iron flywheel is 6000 – it is therefore recommended to change to steel flywheels for all racing and 6000rpm-plus applications.

Cast iron is most frequently used for flywheels, as the machined surface texture of the material is compatible with that used in clutch linings.

Connecting rods

The 335-Series engines used three connecting rods that, although appearing similar, had different centre-to-centre length distances. The low-deck block Australian 302ci connecting rods measured 6.020in. To enable the use of the stock 351ci piston, those employed in the low-deck 351ci engines measured 5.778in, while the tall-deck block 351ciM and 400ci Canadian-made engines used longer 6.580in components. The maximum safe rpm limit for all of these stock connecting rods is 6000rpm, as above this amount, they have a strength restriction in the 'I' beam. Therefore, for rpm over this, it is paramount to fit high-strength aftermarket equivalents.

The big and little end sizes of these connecting rods are identical. The stock tunnel bore diameter size of all Cleveland connecting rods is 2.4362-2.4369in, and with the bearing shells fitted, will fit a nominal $2\frac{5}{16}$in diameter crankshaft big-end journal or, more precisely 2.3100-2.3111in, with a factory recommended running clearance of between 0.001-0.0026in. The bored and honed size of the little end of all connecting rods is 0.9104-0.9112in. The gudgeon pin has a 0.9122-0.9125in diameter, which allows for an 'interference fit' in the connecting rod within the factory tolerance range of 0.0005in, as a minimum to a maximum amount of 0.0013in.

The Boss 351ci connecting rods were made from 1041-H, as were those of the stock production 351ci engine, but, were crack tested, shot peened, and fitted with higher than stock strength connecting rod bolts.

The stock production 351ci-2V, 351ci-4V, and the Boss 351ci connecting rods were never intended to be classed as suitable for racing purposes, and any attempt to use them in these applications would have resulted in a failed engine. This is because the connecting rod tunnel bores would have distorted, and become oval, causing the bearing tunnel bore to follow suit, and the big-end bearing shell surfaces to come into contact with the big-end journals. The connecting rod big-end tunnel bores narrowed across the part-line, which usually affected two, three, or more connecting rods, resulting in a wrecked engine.

As the stock versions were only suitable for use up to, but not exceeding, 6,000rpm which was above the mandatory durability level there was prudent reasoning behind Fords decision to make the Boss 351ci connecting rods.

The current availability of stronger connecting rods superior to the stock production items from aftermarket sources makes them relatively easy to acquire, and it is necessary to use these in any non-stock application, as without them, the risk of failure is too high.

Pistons

The vast majority of Cleveland engines were factory fitted with Autothermic cast aluminium, steel strut pistons that Ford durability tested to 5500rpm. This was just above their point of maximum power and is their recommended limit. However, in some instances, they have been turned to 6000rpm with no ill effects, but due to limited strength, they will only endure this treatment if moderate loading and power is being generated.

The 1971 Boss 351ci-4V engine had 'raised topped' forged/impact extruded TRW pistons, while the 1972-1974 HO 351ci-4V engine was fitted with 'flat topped' TRW forged/impact extruded pistons suitable for 7000rpm operation.

Autothermic means the piston changes shape relative to the heat it contains, and as its temperature increases, the rigidity factor of the two steel struts within the structure causes its ovality to alter. The main purpose of this type of piston is to prevent the engine from having piston skirt to cylinder bore contact, and therefore 'knock' on cold start, and also to avoid any piston skirt scuffing when the piston is hot. As the cost of these components is now relatively low, nowadays for racing purposes where 6000rpm and above is being used, forged pistons and

CLEVELAND V8 ENGINE VARIANTS

aftermarket connecting rods are most commonly used. Fitting these special parts means the engine will be very reliable over a long period, with piston or connecting rod failure extremely unlikely. If the stock connecting rods are to be used, stronger aftermarket hyper-eutectic cast pistons can be employed in conjunction with them, as they are stronger than the Ford or replacement part manufacturer's stock-type cast pistons. However, to avoid connecting rod failure, one of these engines should be limited to 6000rpm.

The majority of present-day enthusiasts using these engines in competition tend to keep the maximum revs between 6000 and 7000rpm, with few wanting to take their engines higher, as although they have the potential to exceed this amount, in most instances there is little need to turn one faster than 7000rpm.

Only the stock connecting rods and cast pistons prevented the stock engine from reliably turning 6000rpm plus, as all other components connected with the bottom end of these engines were very robust. The Ford-published literature clearly stated that the stock engine cast pistons and connecting rods were unsuitable for racing purposes, and that Boss 351ci-4V connecting rods and forged pistons were requisite for such applications, although 6200rpm was the maximum amount for these components if they were to remain durable.

Although all capacity engines can be used for racing purposes as long as suitable rpm limits are observed, nowadays the tendency is to use only the 351ci engines.

The low-deck 351ci will deliver power over a wider rpm band than the 400ci and the 351ciM engines, which have larger diameter main bearings, resulting in a higher bearing speed. This limits their maximum rpm to around 6000.

Although very similar to the 351ci, the Australian 302ci engines have a shorter stroke, and, through having a smaller capacity, do not produce the same power, although they have equal rpm capability. Overall, the 351ci low-deck engine is most often regarded as the best of the Cleveland V8s.

The stroked 351ci (now 382ci) Cleveland V8 as fitted into George Sheweiry's genuine Australian 1978 Falcon Cobra two-door coupé which is seen regularly on New Zealand racing circuits – this car is number 211 of the 400 built.

Chapter 2
Cylinder heads

302CI-2V, 351CI-2V, 351CI-4V, BOSS 351CI-4V, HO 351CI-4V, CJ 351CI-4V, 351MCI-2V, & 400CI-2V

The Cleveland engines employed six distinct designs of production cylinder heads all sharing similar basic cylinder head castings, which meant they were technically interchangeable when fitted onto engine blocks. There were two basic shapes of combustion chamber, either 'open' or 'closed,' which can also be further broken down into two basic versions of each shape.

There is an amount of common use in that the USA-made 351ci-2V, the Australian-made 351ci-2V and 351ci-4V, and the Canadian-made 351ciM-2V and 400ci-2V engines, all shared identical cylinder heads. Of the six factory specification cylinder heads, five originated in the USA, with only the Australian-made 302ci-2V engine cylinder head being unique to Ford Australia. Individually, the five USA-made cylinder heads were the 351ci-2V (1970-1974), 351ci-4V (1970-1971), Cobra Jet 351ci-4V (1971-1974), High Output 351ci-4V (1972-1974), and Boss 351ci-4V (1971).

The second feature, relating to the

Basic 'open' combustion chamber shape.

CYLINDER HEADS

Basic 'closed' combustion chamber shape.

Cleveland cylinder head basic castings, is the difference between the two inlet and exhaust port sizes, and the two inlet and exhaust valve head sizes used on these engines. Coupled with the two quite different combustion chamber shapes, and the two slight variations of each type, with the valves sizes, this amounts to a substantial range of combinations, but are all easily identifiable.

Valve sizes and lengths

The North American 351ci-2V, 351ciM-2V, 400ci-2V, and the Australian 302ci-2V, 351ci-2V and 351ci-4V engine cylinder heads have inlet and exhaust valves sized at 2.040in/51.8mm and 1.650in/41.9mm, which is smaller than those employed in the high-performance oriented Boss, Cobra Jet, and High

This picture shows a 'large' inlet port on the left, and a 'small' inlet port on the right.

THE ESSENTIAL SOURCE BOOK

In this photograph, a 'large' exhaust port can be seen on the left, and a 'small' exhaust port on the right.

Output 351ci-4V engines. They are very generous valve head sizes and possibly the largest ever used for stock production V8 engines of this general capacity range. The 351ci-4V, CJ 351ci-4V, Boss 351ci-4V, and HO 351ci-4V cylinder heads have larger inlet and exhaust valves at 2.190in/55.6mm head diameter inlet valves, and 1.710in/43.4mm head diameter exhaust valves. These are fairly large valves for stock production engines of this capacity, and irrespective of the maker, larger valves are rarely seen fitted in intermediate sized engines.

All Cleveland inlet valves have an overall length of 5.235in/132.9mm, while all exhaust valves are 5.050in/128.3mm, with every one having 0.342in/8.7mm diameter valve stems.

The six port and combustion chamber configurations:

1. The 1970-1974 USA-made 351ci-2V engines were manufactured with 'open' combustion chambers, small valves at 2.040in/51.8mm for the inlets and 1.650in/41.9mm exhausts, small inlet and exhaust ports and the stock, positive stop, non-adjustable rocker arm arrangement to suit hydraulic camshafts. This cylinder head specification was also used on Australian-made 351ci-2V and 351ci-4V, and the Canadian-made 351Mci-2V and 400ci-2V engines.

2. The USA-made 351ci-4V engines, produced between 1970 and 1971 have 'closed' combustion chambers, large valves at 2.190in/55.6mm for the inlets, and 1.710in/43.4mm exhausts, large inlet and exhaust ports, and all have the stock, positive stop, non-adjustable rocker arm arrangement to suit hydraulic camshafts.

3. The 1971 USA-made Boss 351ci-4V heads have 'closed' combustion chambers, large valves at 2.190in/55.6mm inlets, and 1.710in/43.4mm exhausts, large inlet and exhaust ports, large valves the same as the USA 351ci-4V engines, with an adjustable mechanical rocker arm arrangement appropriate for a mechanical camshaft.

4. The USA-made CJ 351ci-4V cylinder heads of 1971-1974 have 'open' combustion chambers, large valves at 2.190in/55.6mm for the inlets, and 1.710in/43.4mm exhausts, large inlet and exhaust ports, and all have the stock, positive stop, non-adjustable rocker arm arrangement to suit hydraulic camshafts.

5. The 1972-1974 USA-made HO 351ci-4V cylinder heads have 'open' combustion chambers, large valves at 2.190in/55.6mm for the inlets and 1.710in/43.4mm exhausts, large inlet and exhaust ports, and an adjustable mechanical rocker arm arrangement suitable for a mechanical camshaft.

6. The Australian 302ci-2V heads made between 1972 and 1982 have 'closed' combustion chambers, small valves at 2.040in/51.8mm for the inlets, and 1.650in/41.9mm exhausts with small inlet and exhaust ports, and all have the stock, positive stop, non-adjustable rocker arm arrangement to suit hydraulic camshafts. The closed combustion chamber, small inlet, and exhaust port sizes of these 302ci-2V cylinder heads makes them easily identifiable.

Valve split locks

Valve collets/keepers/split locks are the same components, but from here on, this text will be referred to as split locks.

There have been two types of factory fitted split locks and valve stem groove arrangements used on Cleveland engines; the multi-groove, and the single-groove valve locking systems. The most commonly encountered is the multi-groove split lock, used in all USA-made 351ci-2V, 351ci-4V, 351Mci-2V, 400ci-2V, CJ 351ci-4V, and Australian-made 302ci-2V, 351ci-2V, and 351ci-4V engines. The 1971 Boss 351ci-4V and the 1972-1974 HO 351ci-4V engines varied, as they had single grooves, which are the type applicable for racing purposes or any applications using above 5500rpm.

Multi-groove split locks

Multi-groove valve stems each have four round grooves which, when fully assembled, allow them to rotate in the split locks when they are firmly held in the valve spring retainer, as there is clearance between the split locks and the valve stem grooves.

That there are four grooves means there are few problems in service, such as high wear of the grooves, although this changes if over 5500rpm is used on a continuous basis. On this system, the split lock ends butt up to each other, when they are fitted into the valve spring retainer. The precision involved in machining the components means the grooves, as machined into the top of the valve stem, are clearanced

CYLINDER HEADS

0.0015-0.002in/0.038-0.05mm to the internal shape of the split locks.

Using seated valve spring pressures of up to 90lb, and up to 285lb of 'over the nose' pressure, and an rpm limit of 5500rpm, the multi-grooved system will not cause abnormal wear to the split lock grooves, as machined into the valve stems. The 351ci-4V CJ took this valve locking system to the reliable limit but, as the grooves flogged out above 5500rpm, were not totally dependable.

Stock Ford single-groove valves

Ford fitted single-groove valves and split locks to the 1971 Boss 351ci-4V and 1972-1974 HO 351ci-4V engines, but this arrangement did not allow the valve stem to turn within the split lock and valve spring retainer assembly, but instead made a more 'solid' assembly that is predominately used in racing engines. Nowadays, the aftermarket industry is the best source for alternative single-groove valves, split locks, and valve spring retainers for all engines intended to be turned over 5500rpm, as this guarantees the reliability of the valve and valve spring retainer locking system for a considerable length of time, and use to 7000rpm, providing both good durability and reliability.

Valve summary

There were three individual types of inlet and exhaust valves used on Cleveland engines. The small 2.040in/51.8mm inlet and 1.650in/41.9mm exhaust valves all came with multi-groove stems to suit multi-groove split locks. The large 2.190in/55.6mm inlet and 1.710in/43.4mm exhaust valves came in two types, one with multi-groove and the other with single-groove stems.

Stock engine valve spring pressures

The following valve spring pressures are for new components at the correct factory-installed heights:

1. 302ci-2V, 351ci-2V, 351Mci-2V, and 400ci-2V engines have 80lb of seated valve spring pressure at the installed height of 1.825in/46.3mm. There is 200-220lb of 'over the nose' valve spring pressure at 0.407in/10.3mm of valve lift at a 1.418in/36.0mm compressed height, and the camshafts are hydraulic.

2. 351ci-4V engines have 85lb of seated valve spring pressure at the installed height of 1.825in/46.3mm, and 250-270lb of 'over the nose' valve spring pressure at 0.427in/10.8mm of valve lift, at a 1.398in/35.5mm compressed height, with hydraulic camshafts.

3. Cobra Jet 351ci-4V engines have 85lb of seated valve spring pressure at the installed height of 1.825in/46.3mm, and 270-285lb of 'over the nose' valve spring pressure at 0.480in/12.2mm valve lift at a 1.345in/34.1mm compressed height. Hydraulic camshaft used.

4. Boss 351ci-4V and High Output 351ci-4V engines have 90lb of seated valve spring pressure at the installed height of 1.825in/46.3mm, and 310-315lb of 'over the nose' valve spring pressure at 0.477in/12.1mm of valve lift, at a 1.348in/34.2mm compressed height, using a mechanical camshaft.

At approximately 5500rpm, all stock production, Cleveland hydraulic lifter, flat tappet, camshaft equipped engines have a propensity to begin suffering from hydraulic lifter 'pump-up,' via the lifter mechanism. A change to anti-pump-up lifters removes this problem, and allows engines to turn 6500rpm, provided that all the valve springs are of a suitable tension.

The multi-grooves as machined in the valve stems 'flog out' within a short time frame, if above 5500rpm is used continuously. Therefore, for guaranteed long-term reliability, for an engine fitted with anti-pump lifters, and any stock Ford-made or aftermarket high-performance hydraulic camshaft, the rpm limit needs to be kept down to this level. The valve spring pressure required in this situation would be in the vicinity of 85lb when seated, and 250lb 'over the nose,' irrespective of the maximum valve lift, which is more or less the stock amount of valve spring pressure used in a 351ci-4V engine.

In order to avoid problems involving the valve stem grooves flogging out when turning to 5500rpm plus in high-performance, hydraulic lifter, and camshaft applications, it is necessary to change to single-groove valves, single-groove split locks, and steel valve spring retainers. This is precisely the arrangement Ford fitted as stock to the Boss 351ci-4V engines made for 1971, and the HO 351ci-4V engines, as made between 1972 and 1974, which were equipped with a mechanical camshaft.

Left-to-right, standard pressed steel rocker arm, cast fulcrum, oil jet deflector-washer and securing screw.

THE ESSENTIAL SOURCE BOOK

It is recommended that an engine equipped with an hydraulic lifter camshaft is turned to a maximum of 6500rpm, and, for a mechanical camshaft-equipped engine 7000rpm, although some drivers have turned their racing engines to as much as 7200-7500rpm, with no ill effects.

When fitted to 351ci engines, the maximum power for 351ci-4V cylinder heads is between 7000 and 7200rpm, which is much the same as many other two-valve per cylinder wedge-type combustion chamber engines.

Without a doubt, the 1971 model year Boss 351ci-4V engine cylinder heads, with adjustable valve train to suit mechanical camshafts, were the highest stock specification available. This was followed by the USA-made 1970-1971 model year 351ci-4V engine heads, with non-adjustable valve train to suit hydraulic camshafts, which, having the same basic casting, made conversion to the Boss 351ci-4V specification relatively easy.

Although now rare, the 1970-1971 model year 351ci-4V cylinder heads are available, and any keen enthusiast will be able acquire a pair, although should be prepared to pay a fairly high price. However, on the basis of being stock production cast iron cylinder heads, which, with very little preparation allow good engine power to be generated, they are excellent value for money. Anyone wanting to run an all cast iron engine in a racing application needs to find, and use, a good set of these 'closed' chamber cylinder heads.

In reality, the 1972-1974 model year HO 351ci-4V engine was the replacement for the 1971 Boss 351ci-4V phased out at the end of that car model year. The difference was a lower compression, because of the switch to low lead fuel, and reduced octane ratings via the open combustion chamber, and milder camshaft timing, although the valve train was still mechanical, and to the same specification as the Boss 351ci-4V.

The aftermarket industry now provides proven high strength components to make totally reliable valve trains for all these engines, and many such companies make racing quality single groove inlet and exhaust valves, split locks, valve spring retainers, valve springs, guide-plates, rocker studs,

Standard rocker arm position at zero valve lift. Point of contact with the tip of the valve stem is now biased to the left-hand side of the valve stem tip.

In this photograph, the standard rocker arm is positioned at 0.550in valve lift. The point of contact with the top of the tip is now biased to the right-hand side of the valve stem tip.

and rocker arms; today, all manner of top quality, almost indestructible parts can be acquired from these sources at a reasonable cost.

Rocker arms
The standard pressed steel rocker arms with cast fulcrums and extremely robust securing screws are ideal for all hydraulic lifter applications. When in the regular position, as the tip of the rocker arm that contacts the tip of the valve stem is exceptionally well shaped, it can easily accommodate valve lifts up to 0.0550in plus. It is both unnecessary and undesirable to re-position the rocker

CYLINDER HEADS

This picture illustrates the pushrod guide plate and screw-in rocker stud system employed in the cylinder head of an engine equipped with a mechanical camshaft.

arm when the valve lift is altered from the standard amount.

Generally speaking, 'anti-pump-up' hydraulic lifters are required for any rpm over roughly 5500; the Iskenderian 382-HY items are an excellent choice. The recommended lifter pre-load is 0.020in, and while the rocker arm position needs to remain fixed, non-standard length pushrods may be required to ensure the amount is maintained. Although Ford does not supply these components, they are readily available from aftermarket sources, as are push rod kits which allow any length pushrod to be made to suit individual applications.

Engines equipped with mechanical camshafts used the same type of rocker arm, and although the fulcrums were similar, they were located on parallel shank rocker studs, allowing them to become height adjustable; the rocker arms were also pushrod guided, as opposed to the fulcrum being fixed to the cylinder head casting. The cylinder heads were machined to house pushrod guide plates and screw-in rocker arm studs. Provided that the pushrods are an appropriate length to ensure the rocker arm geometry remains within the factory requirements, any Cleveland engine can be machined to suit a mechanical camshaft; it is mandatory that the rocker arm to meets the criteria shown in the two preceding photographs.

Chapter 3

Preparing Cleveland V8 short blocks for racing

The problems with the stock short assembly are confined to six basic areas; namely, the stock-connecting rods, the oiling system, cylinder bore wall thickness, pistons, camshaft skew gear oiling, and the main caps fretting in the block registers. Requirements for improved reliability include connecting rod centre-to-centre distance lengths, connecting rod bolts, refurbishing stock-connecting rods, connecting rod cap modifications, fitting four-bolt main caps to two-bolt blocks, fitting liners and Plateau-honing the cylinder bore wall.

CONNECTING RODS

When, in the 1970s, the 351ci-2V and 351ci-4V engines fitted with stock components were first altered for racing purposes, they were adequately strong to withstand 6000rpm, which for a standard component engine was quite acceptable, and similar to other comparable engines. However, in the long-term, for sustained 6000rpm operation, the stock cast pistons proved to be a weak link, and most engines were fitted with forged pistons to avoid possible failure. Today, hypereutectic pistons are sufficient for prolonged 6000rpm use in 351ci-2V or 351ci-4V engines, with a bottom end equipped with stock components.

In spite of Ford's recommendation that alternative high strength connecting rods were necessary for racing, many enthusiasts were determined to use the stock components, and although these engines were powerful, they were also fragile, and gained the unjustifiable reputation of being weak. This vulnerability due to connecting rod failure was therefore not an engine fault, as such, but more a case of being fitted with internal components unsuitable for the application. Ford never saw any reason to make stock road-going engines sufficiently strong for racing purposes, but, produced engines that met their reliability and durability levels at the lowest possible cost.

The stock Cleveland connecting rods were perfectly satisfactory to 6000rpm, however, if the engine exceeded this amount and reached 7000rpm, after the third or fourth time this occurred, the bearings failed, as the big-end bearings 'nipped' onto the crankshaft big-end journal. This was because the connecting rod tunnel bore distorted under the loading, and became oval, reducing the width across its part-line. Although all eight connecting rod big-end bearings would be seriously affected, normally two or three seized simultaneously, causing the engine to stop. Although building ovality into the connecting rod big-end tunnel bore addressed this problem, brand new connecting rods would eventually break in the 'I' beam, approximately 1in below the gudgeon pin, after around four hours use, up to 7000rpm, which cannot be regarded as long-term reliability.

When, in the 1970s, the stock pistons and connecting rods proved unreliable at any rpm over 6000, the Ford-recommended solution was to replace them with the Boss 351ci items, which were tested by Ford as suitable up to 8000rpm.

Only these components lack the basic strength required to build a very strong Cleveland V8 short assembly, and brand new extremely robust aftermarket connecting rods and forged pistons are now readily available at a reasonable cost, making it pointless to chance the high risk of losing an entire engine, simply for the price of a set.

It is essential that any stock-connecting rod, intended for a maximum 6000rpm, has the small-end diameter

PREPARING CLEVELAND V8 SHORT BLOCKS FOR RACING

checked, to ensure it is to factory size, before being both straightness and crack tested. After this, if the components are found satisfactory, the connecting rod and cap matching surfaces can be re-machined, new connecting rod bolts fitted, and finally the big-end bearing tunnel bores resized. The high cost of this work makes the price of brand new rods look attractive, and many enthusiasts simply buy them as opposed to refurbishing what are now old and, possibly fatigued, original components. Reasonably priced New Old Stock (NOS) connecting rods are available from internet auction sites, and can be extremely good value for money, as they will not be fatigued and generally need no refurbishment, although the tunnel bore must always be checked for size before installation.

High strength aftermarket connecting rods are also available in many styles and centre-to-centre distances, and have become much less expensive since the 1990s. It is now common practice to replace the stock connecting rods, which are 5.778in/146.8mm centre-to-centre distance, with those measuring 6.000in/152.4mm used in conjunction with quite lightweight, 'squat' style, custom made, forged pistons.

It is important for enthusiasts to be cautious when intending to use slipper skirt pistons on Cleveland blocks, as this can lead to excessive bore wear on the thrust side of each cylinder, meaning that 'full skirt' design pistons will prove beneficial to bore wear. If the skirt design is insubstantial, and/or if the piston to bore clearance is excessive, bores can become unserviceable within a very short time. This type of piston is therefore unsuitable for use in the Cleveland V8 engine, and more full skirt is highly recommended.

The full-skirted forged pistons can weigh as little as 500g for the piston, and 100g for the gudgeon pin, giving a total weight of 600g, and a saving of up to 100g over the stock items. An engine rebalance is obviously required when components like this are changed, and when this is done, it is advisable to reduce the amount of 'external balance,' as found on the crankshaft damper and flywheel, as opposed to removing material from the counterweights.

CLEVELAND V8 CONNECTING ROD CENTRE-TO-CENTRE DISTANCE LENGTHS

The Cleveland V8 engines used connecting rods with three stock lengths; 6.020in for the Australian 302ci, 5.778in for all USA- and Australian-made 351ci, and 6.580in for the Canadian-made 351ciM and 400ci engines. There has been a definite leaning towards the use of connecting rods longer than stock, but there is a limit to this trend, and it should not simply be regarded as 'the longer the better.'

In the very early 1960s, Engine Engineer, Ed Pinkerton, worked for Ford's 'Scientific Research Organisation,' located opposite the EEE building on Oakwood Boulevard, where Car Styling and Body Engineering was housed, which afforded him the opportunity to work on various theoretical and practical engineering matters, beneficial to the company's future projects. Ed Pinkerton carried out significant experimental work, in order to separate fact from fiction, and to determine the ideal connecting rod-to-stroke ratios, in a quest to obtain optimum engine efficiency. Much of his investigation involved a single-cylinder test engine, and, later, the FE NASCAR engines, resulting in the production of a range of interchangeable connecting rod and piston combinations, specifically for these tests. The sets of connecting rods were approximately 0.030in/0.75mm different from each other, in centre-to-centre length. They were used in conjunction with pistons, with the gudgeon pin re-positioned to compensate, allowing the overall piston crown to remain constant. Using the same two cars and engines, all combinations were track-tested, resulting in irrefutable conclusions.

The 1.68:1-1.72:1 connecting rod-to-stroke ratio combinations worked most effectively, and although the horsepower and torque remained more or less constant for all engines, there was a significant difference in the rate of acceleration off or out of a turn in a test car.

The problem with connecting rod-to-stroke ratios larger than 1.72:1 is that, as the combustion pressure increases when the piston is at top dead centre and just past it, the connecting rod is technically pushing down vertically onto the crankshaft. The longer the connecting rod, the longer the time it is effectively too vertical, and, as a result, the combustion pressure energy is not being used to maximum efficiency to turn the crankshaft in the direction of rotation; essentially it is trying to push the crankshaft out of the bottom of the engine.

The experiments carried out by Ed Pinkerton concluded that, generally, for all current Ford engines, a connecting rod centre-to-centre distance to crankshaft stroke ratio between 1.68:1 and 1.72:1 was the requirement, with the latter regarded as optimum. The centre-to-centre distance of the connecting rod is divided by the stroke of the engine, which is sometimes referred to as the 'L over R' of an engine. Pinkerton noted that if the connecting rod-to-stroke ratio was less than 1.68:1, this factor did not necessarily result in an engine lacking responsiveness, however it did start to affect the piston skirt service life; the shorter the connecting rod, the higher the rate of piston skirt/bore wall wear.

Ford sometimes went beyond the ideal connecting rod-to-stroke ratio of 1.72:1 for other reasons, notably for the 1969 and 1970 Boss 302ci Trans-Am racing engines, that used its Indianapolis racing engine connecting rods, with a 5.312in centre-to-centre distance. This was coupled with the 3in stroke, which, quite coincidentally also resulted in a ratio of 1.77:1. In this instance, it was exceeded to keep the piston weight down, as 0.157in of connecting rod 'I' beam cross sectional area weighed less than 0.157in of aluminium piston skirt mass, but, this ratio was regarded as the absolute upper limit. In the 1960s, car engines were not reaching such high rpm levels as today, where current NASCAR V8 engines are turning 9000rpm, and, based on experimentation and the subsequent results, all have connecting rod-to-stroke ratios in the vicinity of 1.77:1-1.81:1.

To increase the capacity, nowadays, various types of long-stroke crankshafts are fitted to V8 engines, and as a result, the connecting rods are becoming shorter and the pistons designed more squat to fit into the block. Although this procedure is quite acceptable, due to the loading, the bore wall and piston skirt life can be greatly reduced. Therefore, it becomes a matter of obtaining a larger

THE ESSENTIAL SOURCE BOOK

capacity with a reduced service life expectancy over stock, and possibly, an engine with less than ideal engine performance characteristics.

The original low-deck USA-made 1970-1974 351ci-2V and 351ci-4V engines used 5.778in centre-to-centre distance length connecting rods, as did the Australian-made 351ci-2V and 351ci-4V engines between 1972 and 1982. However, the 302ci engines manufactured at the Australian Geelong Engine Plant between 1972 and 1982 used components with a centre-to-centre distance of 6.020in, specifically to allow them to employ the 351ci piston. This move, while allowing Ford Australia to use a common part, reduced engine performance capability, as the connecting rod-to-stroke ratio was well above the ideal range.

When the 351ciM-2V engines came on stream in the mid-1970s, they were used to power trucks and many cars. Mrs Lee Iacocca had a car fitted with one of these engines which cut out on the over-run, leading up to a roundabout. When the engine stalled, there was limited power assistance for the steering, and she careered straight over the roundabout and into a fruit stall in a market place, before coming to a halt. Fortunately, no one was injured, but on hearing of the accident her husband, President of Ford, Lee Iacocca, demanded the problem was fixed immediately, as it was unacceptable for expensive Lincoln cars to stall in this way. Engine Engineering engineer Bill Barr was assigned to investigate the problem, and when testing the cars, could not believe how sluggish they were in comparison to the earlier USA 351ci Cleveland engines. He subsequently made enquires into the differences between the two versions. When he was given the data, he recalled remarks made by Ed Pinkerton at a lunchtime discussion in 1963, during the Indy engine programme, regarding connecting rod-to-stroke ratios. He noted the long connecting rod aspect of the 351ciM-2V engine and extra weight of the internal components, in comparison to the 351ci US Cleveland. The connecting rod-to-stroke ratio of the USA 351ci Cleveland was 1.65:1, versus 1.88:1 of the 351ciM.

For low-deck block 351ci racing engine applications, changing the original stock-connecting rod centre-to-centre distance length from 5.778in to 6.020in, in conjunction with the stock

Oil goes across the front of the engine block, as indicated by the two arrows.

PREPARING CLEVELAND V8 SHORT BLOCKS FOR RACING

351ci stroke, results in an increase in a ratio from 1.65:1 to an ideal 1.72:1.

Connecting rod-to-stroke ratios

Engine	Connecting rod-to-stroke ratio
302ci low-deck	2.01:1
351ci low-deck	1.65:1
351ci tall-deck	1.88:1
400ci tall-deck	1.65:1

Kits to suit a mechanical camshaft-equipped engine are available from Moroso, under part number MOR-22050. The four 5/16in grub screws have a 3/64in diameter hole through the centre, and the 3/8in grub screw has one of 1/16in.

UPRATING THE CLEVELAND OILING SYSTEM

Although the earlier design small-block Ford V8 engine has a simply excellent oiling system, the one employed on the Cleveland V8 is not as satisfactory, as it has a few problems for high rpm work. Also, any engine turning more than 5500rpm necessitates fitting an 'oil restrictor kit,' which is a fairly simple procedure, and improves the oiling for up to 7000rpm operation, for both wet and dry sump engines. These are available from various sources, including Moroso and Summit, and restrict the amount of oil going to the camshaft bearings, and the left hand side lifter gallery.

The oiling system in the stock Cleveland engine picks up the oil from the very bottom of the oil pan, and draws into the oil pump immersed in the reservoir, before routing it through the oil filter and back into the block main oil feed gallery, which is much the same as the small-block Ford. However, the similarities end at this point.

The main gallery, with a 1/2in diameter hole, goes across the front of the block, directly above the foremost main bearing, and under the front camshaft bearing, where it intersects with another 1/2in diameter oil gallery that feeds oil down to the front main bearing and up to the left hand lifter gallery (to the left when facing the front of the engine). There is also a 1/4in diameter hole, feeding oil to the front camshaft bearing, within this front-positioned oil circuitry.

The lifter gallery extends all the way to the back of the block, and while it feeds the eight lifters on that side of the engine, it also feeds oil down to the four rear-most main bearings in the block, which are also fed oil individually from those main bearings up to the camshaft bearings immediately above them. At the rear of the engine block, the lifter gallery feeds oil down to the main bearing, through an 11/32in diameter hole, then up to the camshaft bearing through a 1/4in diameter hole. Here, another gallery 11/32in in diameter feeds oil up to the right hand lifter gallery; these three holes are grouped very closely together in the rear main bearing tunnel bore of the block. When applied to a road-going engine, this system is perfectly acceptable, but, for High-performance engines turning over 6000rpm, it can be improved on the basis of main bearing oiling. This also means improved big-end bearing oiling, which is achieved through both receiving priority oil flow by restricting it to the camshaft bearings, and right hand lifter gallery.

To ensure optimum oil flow to the main and big-end bearings, while maintaining near uniform pressure within the entire oiling system to the engine, the oil flow within the Cleveland block can be restricted in six areas, which are the five camshaft bearings, and the right hand side of the block lifter gallery, as viewed when facing the front of the engine. Fitting a grub screw with a small diameter hole through the centre, sized at either 3/64 or 1/16in will limit the flow.

The size of the rear oil gallery hole that feeds oil to the right hand side lifter gallery is dependent on whether the camshaft is mechanical or hydraulic. The 1/16in diameter hole is suitable for an engine equipped with a mechanical camshaft, but not necessarily totally appropriate, if a hydraulic camshaft is used, as it may not allow sufficient oil to pass, thereby overly restricting the flow, preventing correct lifter function. This, in turn, may cause the lifters to bleed down on that side, making a clattering sound and a simultaneous loss of engine power. An engine employing a hydraulic camshaft needs diameter hole sizes ranging from 1/8 to 3/16in.

The oil flow is reduced by the use of smaller holes, however, if the oil contains particles, the risk of blockage becomes increased, but with their use, superior excessive oil flow restriction is obviously achieved; the larger holes used within the range, the less risk of obstruction. The available kits mostly supply the small-holed component with the maximum size used in the restrictor plugs of 3/32in.

Fitting a foremost main bearing to a camshaft bearing restrictor plug is a little more complicated than straight drilling and tapping a hole and fitting a grub screw, because it has to be fitted deeper into the block, compared to the second, third, fourth, and fifth main bearing to camshaft drillings. Because of this, the foremost camshaft bearing does not normally have a restrictor placed in its oil feed hole; as an alternative option, a restrictor grub screw with a 3/64in diameter hole can be fitted low down in the block. To do this, the existing drilled 1/4in hole, which goes to the camshaft bearing, is tapped 5/16in UNC through into the second part of the 1/4in diameter camshaft bearing oil feed hole, close to the camshaft bearing. The difficulty here lies with the ability to tap a hole this deep into the block, using a stock-sized tap. Long series taps, with smaller than normal shanks, are available for carrying out this type of work, but are generally only available from specialist engineering supply stores. Taps of this type allow both the first and second parts of the hole to be tapped quite easily. To fit the foremost grub screw, it must be

THE ESSENTIAL SOURCE BOOK

The foremost camshaft oil feed restrictor is positioned reasonably deep in the front of the block, as indicated by the arrow.

wound down through the first part of the threaded hole, wound out of this hole, across the gallery, and started in the second portion of the drilling. To prevent the grub screw falling off the Allen key, the block is simply turned upside down, so that the grub screw can be started in the second part of the drilled and tapped hole in the block; when the thread bottoms out, it is firmly tightened.

The block oil gallery must be thoroughly cleaned to remove all traces of swarf, produced from tapping the holes.

To isolate the back of the foremost main bearing shell from the oil flow, an additional un-drilled grub screw can also be fitted into the first portion of the camshaft oil feed hole.

The larger ⅜in grub screw is positioned in the gallery, extending from the rear main to the right-hand lifter gallery, which, when facing the front of the engine, is to the right. This oil gallery has an ¹¹⁄₃₂in diameter, and the grub screw limits the amount of oil flowing to the eight lifters on that side of the engine.

The grub screws fixed into the oil galleries that individually limit the oil flow to the second, third, fourth, and fifth camshaft bearings, and the one restricting the amount directed to the right-hand side lifter gallery, must be below the surface of the main bearing tunnel bore surface. Otherwise, they will interfere with the fit of the main bearing shell inserts into the block. The holes are tapped into the oil galleries, using either an intermediate or a taper tap. Using an Allen key, each grub screw is tightened firmly into each threaded hole. To prevent any possibility of them coming loose during service, a locking agent, such as Loctite 256, is often advised. However, this is a matter of preference, as after doing this, it will usually prove very difficult to remove the grub screw, at such times as when the block is cleaned during a future rebuild.

As fitting the foremost oil gallery restrictor plug is not a straightforward process, it can be considered optional. The oiling system will be satisfactory with either five or six restrictor grub screws fitted, with no serious alterations to the block.

All these procedures should be followed to attain the ability to turn one of these engines, using a wet sump to 7000rpm, which is sufficient for most applications. Large capacity wet sumps and pickup pipes are readily available from the aftermarket industry.

PREPARING CLEVELAND V8 SHORT BLOCKS FOR RACING

The other four camshaft bearing restrictor plugs are positioned adjacent to the main bearing oil feed holes, as indicated by the four arrows.

FOUR-BOLT MAIN CAP 351CI BLOCKS

The vast majority of Cleveland engines have two-bolt main caps, and, due to the numbers available, many are now used in racing applications. However, when turning one of these engines above 6000rpm, an amount of fretting is for the most part unavoidable. Fretting is the deterioration of the surfaces of the block register and main caps, due to the micro-movement of the main caps against the machined block register surface, while the engine is in operation. The micro-movement, which can be very destructive, is caused by the various forces going into the block structure, versus the basic strength and location of the main caps. As the engine was primarily designed for standard road use, in this capacity, it showed no signs of either durability or reliability problems, and these matters only came to the fore when it was applied to competition situations.

Over the years, in a bid to prevent main caps fretting against the block registers on V8 engines, all manner of technology has been tried, but it has never been as straightforward as it may have first appeared, as there are several other factors involved. Namely, the method by which they are secured and located to the block, either using two or four bolts, register, and/or dowel location. In the case of the Cleveland V8 engine, all main caps are register located, and can employ either a two- or four-bolt securing, although the latter is preferable; as a means of achieving increased strength, main caps are often made using nodular iron.

The method by which the crankshaft is counterweighted is very significant, and to quote ex-Chief Engineer of the Engine and Foundry Division of the Ford Motor Company, Hank Lenox, who re-designed the small-block 289ci crankshafts in 1967, when Ford was having block problems on the GT-40 programme, "A conventional dual plane crankshaft for a V8 engine can be designed in one of two ways, for maximum bob-weight or minimum bearing loading. The maximum bob-weight type of crankshaft tends to cause the bearing loads to be very high on the 2nd and 4th main bearings." The maximum bob-weight configuration crankshaft tends to be the favoured design, as not only is it cheaper to produce, it is very suitable for the amount of rpm required for a stock engine. The failure of all 13 small-block engines at Le Mans in 1967, when block breakage occurred, led to the pursuit of 100 per cent reliability, and as a result, the new crankshaft was counterweighted differently, to reduce the loading on

THE ESSENTIAL SOURCE BOOK

the 2nd and 4th block main bearing bulkheads. This measure was successful, as the 1968 and 1969 Le Mans race results proved.

The stock 289ci or 302ci engine block, used in conjunction with a Boss 302ci crankshaft, has the lowest possible failure rate because of the reduced loadings on the main bearing web bulkheads, although, there is obviously a limitation with any stock production block used for competition purposes. However, using this combination maximises its reliability.

Crankshafts of this design configuration, suitable for Cleveland engines, are available from Ford and aftermarket outlets, and although the cost may be a drawback, are ideal for use in either block. When using Cleveland blocks for racing purposes, it is advisable to use four-bolt main caps, as the two extra bolts help towards the prevention of micro-movement, although they may not totally eliminate the problem.

To attain increased strength, all main caps were made using Ford's 80 per cent nodular iron, and all blocks had sufficient material as cast in the main bearing web areas, allowing for the two extra bolts to be screwed into a well supported structure.

Although the clamping power achieved using four-bolts was substantial, in an effort to stabilise the longitudinal positioning of the three centre main caps in the block, with the objective of preventing any possible main cap movement, Ford went a step further, by employing two close fitting dowels on each.

A further example of the use of this type of crankshaft is the 1969-1970 Boss 302ci small-block engines, which were equipped with four-bolt main caps on the centre three main bearings, while retaining the stock two-bolt components at the front and rear. The crankshaft used was the same design as the Le Mans engines of 1968 and 1969. The Boss 302ci crankshaft design reduced the bearing loading, by having the third counterweight in from the front and rear positioned 90 degrees to the first and second, in from each end of the crankshaft, and, the third in from the end were phased at 180 degrees to each other. From the counterweight positioning perspective, the GT-40 up-date 289ci/Boss 302ci component is excellent for racing applications. It is important to realise that, although all crankshafts may appear the same, in actuality they are not, and distinguishing the differences takes careful scrutiny.

This 351ci Cleveland block displays significant fretting of the main bearing registers, particularly around the threaded holes, and remedial machine work will soon be essential.

PREPARING CLEVELAND V8 SHORT BLOCKS FOR RACING

Substantial four-bolt main cap and bolts.

When used in racing applications, a two-bolt main cap Cleveland block employing a standard crankshaft will almost certainly exhibit signs of fretting, if it is turned above 6000rpm. After around 2000 racing miles, it will reach a critical stage, necessitating remedial machine work to remove the effects or, in a worse case scenario, could be written-off. On the other hand, up to 6500rpm, four-bolt main caps are more resistant to this problem, although after this amount of rpm, they too will also require corrective machine work in due course.

It should be noted that few, if any, Boss 302ci engine blocks and main caps exhibited any sign of main cap to block fretting, even after thousands of miles of normal or hard racing use, which is partly due to the very strong block, robust main caps, solid main cap to block securing, and dowel location. The reduced bearing loading design of crankshaft, which determines the impact of the crankshaft design, should not be underestimated. Although costly, all components employed in this engine were high specification, designed specifically for high-performance and racing applications.

To restore the block and main cap to original factory specifications, the damaged surfaces can be re-machined, although this process can only be carried out once or twice. The procedure entails removing a minimum amount of material from the base of the main caps, and block register surfaces, thereby restoring them to an as new condition. There is, however, a problem with this course of action – if too much material is removed from the block, the camshaft to crankshaft centre distance decreases, slackening the timing chain, and if this situation worsens, the more the block is machined. However, if a gear drive is used, no problem occurs as the tooth mesh can be reset. When the block register and main cap matching surfaces have been reground, the main bearing tunnel bores are align-honed, to restore the required minimum main bearing tunnel bore diameter size of 2.9417in.

Four-bolt blocks are safe and present no problems to 6500rpm, on the basis of bottom-end strength and main cap movement, with all five main caps having four-bolts; two ½in and two ⅜in diameter bolts per cap. The caps, like the two-bolt blocks, are located in registers without dowels. The extra two bolts per main cap give superior clamping power, to hold it in position against the block to resist micro-movement.

The register width across the block

THE ESSENTIAL SOURCE BOOK

is identical for both four- and two-bolt blocks and all are identically cast with an adequate amount of material, to allow drilling and tapping to accommodate the two outer ⅜in UNC bolts. The four-bolt main cap blocks have considerable clamping power, holding the caps against the block, and are usually quite sufficient to prevent main cap micro-movement to the reasonable figure of 6500rpm. It is possible for any two-bolt block to be fitted with a set of four-bolt main caps, and for all intents and purposes, be correctly termed a four-bolt main cap block. However, a block like this would need to be line-bored/align-honed after they have been fitted. Four-bolt main caps can be acquired from scrapped or damaged blocks, and aftermarket suppliers.

BORE WALL THICKNESS

As it is quite possible to inspect 20 or 30 blocks, without finding one with uniformly thick bore walls, it is imperative for any stock production 'low-deck' block being prepared for competition to have all the bores in the block ultrasonically tested for bore wall thickness, before being re-bored, and many engine re-conditioners have the specialised equipment for this purpose.

The mandatory factory 'thin-wall' casting specification was for a minimum uniform bore wall thickness of 0.160in, plus 0.020in and minus nothing, which was difficult to achieve on a production basis using sand casting moulds, as this technique relied on repeated accurate placement of precision-made cores. Difficulties arose, as the water jacket cores were not always positioned accurately in relation to other areas of the mould, and with the added problem of them shifting during the pouring process, often resulted in some blocks having irregular or insufficient wall thickness after machining.

In the worst case scenario, one or more bore walls could have a portion of the wall thickness down to around 0.060-0.070in/1.5-1.8mm, while directly opposite this thin area, it could be in the region of 0.260in/6.6mm.

Note: Avoid using any block which may have thin section bore walls (0.060-0.080in/1.5-2.0mm – before or after boring), if the component is intended for use in racing applications.

This can be very hazardous, as the bore wall will most likely crack vertically in this thinnest part, most particularly if this area is on the thrust side. However, the majority of blocks are not this badly affected, and have a minimum bore wall thickness in the region of 0.080-0.120in/2.0-3.0mm. Most cylinders can be re-bored 0.020in, 0.030in, 0.040in, and 0.060in/0.50mm, 0.75mm, 0.10mm, and 1.50mm oversize, by taking no more than 0.002-0.005in/0.051-0.127mm of material away from the thin area of the bore wall, after the thin sections have been established by ultrasonic testing.

Although entailing extra work and additional costs, the block reliability can be improved if each bore is 'off-set bored.' In many cases, the minimum bore wall thickness will be in the region of 0.100in/2.5mm, but even in these instances, particularly for a racing engine block, it is most advisable to reposition the bore/bores to maintain this minimum thickness; the thrust side of each bore is critical, and if they can all be made 0.120in/3.0mm thick, there is every probability of achieving long-term reliability.

When a block is ultrasonically tested, each bore position is marked for its 'new' location, either closer to or further away from the lifter valley, and/or left or right of the original point longitudinally on the block, as in a combination of both axes. There are various ways of determining and finalising the 'new' cylinder axis positioning, and every bore in the block could finally become positioned differently from standard, either up, down or sideways. This is perfectly acceptable, and a machinist practised in block boring will have no trouble undertaking this task.

The thrust faces of the V8 engine cylinder bores are on the left of each bore, when viewed from the front of the block, and keeping these sides of the cylinder bores at the maximum possible thickness, conducive to a minimum of 0.100in/2.5mm elsewhere, is the requirement for optimum reliability.

Although this may appear to involve needless extra effort and expense, it is the only route to follow to make a Cleveland engine as reliable and trouble free as possible. There is little point in failing to observe these procedures if the engine is likely to fail on this basis, making it necessary to repeat the entire procedure with another block. As it entails careful precise work, it is essential to find a vigilant engine re-conditioner sympathetic to your requirements.

It should be noted that using slipper skirt-type pistons is not recommended in these engines, but instead, the full skirt-type. Venolia Pistons, in the USA, custom makes full-skirt forged pistons for these engines to order from its premises in Los Angeles, and can be contacted on telephone numbers: 323-636-9329 or 562-531-8463 and by e-mail: venoliap@aol.com or visit the web site at www.venolia.com for further details.

BLOCKS FITTED WITH LINERS

If a block is to be sleeved, the damaged bore/bores should be ultrasonically tested to establish its approximate centre in relation to the water jacket coring.

In an effort to maintain the overall block casting strength and integrity, the block can then be bored to both accommodate the liner surrounded by the maximum possible uniform wall thickness. When the ideal bore centre position has been charted, the block is machined to take an approximate 0.080in/2.0mm wall thickness liner, which for a standard bore block, means the cylinder is bored to 4.1580-4.1585in/105.6005-105.6132mm. A 4.160in/105.664mm outside diameter liner is then fitted into the block, with a 0.0015-0.002in/0.0381-0.0508mm interference fit.

The existing bores are not normally through bored, but stepped at the bottom, although they can also be stepped at the top of the block with a 'flanged liner.' This means that the machining of both the liner and block must be absolutely precise, if both machined edges are to butt when finally fitted and seated. Before fitting, the liners should be frozen using liquid nitrogen, and the block warmed, using a steam cleaner. After the initial fitting, the liners are then pressed, to ensure they are fully seated onto the machined step, after which the block decks are machined, the bore edges chamfered, and the liners honed.

PREPARING CLEVELAND V8 SHORT BLOCKS FOR RACING

A block without liners is a more solid structure, with better heat conductivity to the water jacket, therefore having them fitted can be a disadvantage, as it results in a barrier between the two components, reducing the heat dissipation, conductivity, and overall strength.

BORE WALL SURFACE FINISH

Irrespective of which piston rings are to be used, to guarantee the best possible ring to bore wall seal, ideally the bore walls need to be 'plateau honed.' To achieve this bore wall finish, the surface is machine-honed finished to 280 grit, then 500 grit, before finally being plateau-honed, using the designated 'corkings' or 'brushes.' However, if this system is used, minimal compression leakage is possible when the engine has been 'run in' or 'bedded in.' Many engine re-conditioners have specialised honing equipment for performing this undertaking, and the bore wall finish is critical in attaining the best possible 'leak down' rates. It is possible to get conventional gapped Moly piston rings reduced to a minimal 2-4 per cent 'leak down' rate, using the plateau-honing technique, and on condition that the rings seat correctly. The resulting power generation will be excellent.

One possible drawback associated with plateau-honed bores is piston rings that do not seat after a small amount of running, as the bore walls become glazed, but this situation is completely preventable. To avoid this problem, the engine should be under loading within 20 seconds of firing, which is relatively easy to do on an engine or chassis dynamometer, and not difficult with the engine fitted in a car, provided that preparation is made to move off immediately.

The thin consistency of 20 weight automatic transmission fluid makes it the recommended choice for lubricating pistons, piston skirts, and bores during engine assembly. The block bore walls should be sprayed liberally with either of these two products, with any residual oil simply allowed to run off the surfaces. Conventional 30 or 40 weight engine oil, especially a friction modified type, should never be used on pistons or rings or when fitting these components into the bores, as it can be the cause of poor ring seating and bore wall glazing. When the pistons have been fitted, and the connecting rod bolts tensioned, there will, however, be an amount of ring drag noise as the engine is turned over by hand, but this is normal and perfectly acceptable.

Initially using a 30 weight monograde, or running in oil in the engine, should be considered, to facilitate correct ring seating and for running-in purposes. Within roughly 20 seconds of the engine firing, it needs to be placed under an amount of loading, with the rpm kept in the vicinity of 1500, while it warms up. It should not exceed 3000rpm for the first hour of running.

To prevent cylinder wall glazing when an engine is installed in a car, it is necessary to put it under an amount of loading almost immediately. Allowing the engine to turn over out of gear, or blipping the throttle to give it some revs, will possibly lead to poor ring seating. This running-in criteria is based on having the engine under some loading, as opposed to the free revving state or using high rpm at any stage of bedding in the rings.

Irrespective of whether the engine is on an engine dynamometer, rolling road or in a car being driven, it should not be run for more than ten minutes, before stopping and being allowed to cool down for approximately one hour. Then repeat the cycle, and after one hour of total running, the oil can be changed for a 50 weight, 20/50 weight mineral or synthetic racing oil. Following the removal of the oil, it should be checked to verify it contains no particles, which would indicate mechanical problems. The engine should then be run for a further 30 minutes in three separate 10-minute sessions, with between 30 and 45 minutes break between each, using up to 4500rpm. Check for abnormal engine noise and coolant leaks throughout the entire process. A keen watch must be kept on both oil and coolant temperatures, which should not be allowed exceed the recommended maximums, under any circumstances.

The optimum coolant temperature for these Ford V8 engines is about 75°C. Above 80-85°C, the power begins reducing, to the extent that, by 100-110°C, an engine could possibly lose between 5 and 10 per cent power. The optimum oil temperature is around 75°C/167F, although 80-85°C is acceptable for mineral based oil. However, the upper limit is 85°C, and if the temperature reaches 90°C, the engine must be shut down, as at this level the oil oxidises and loses lubrication properties. Although the optimum temperature is about 75°C, synthetic oils will allow temperatures of 120-125°C plus/248-257F plus to be used with relative safety; synthetic oils have become more commonly used because of this characteristic.

RE-USING STOCK-CONNECTING RODS

The stock Cleveland connecting rods are very sturdy items, and if 6000rpm is the maximum requirement, it is unnecessary to use anything stronger.

Old pistons can be removed from connecting rods by pressing the gudgeon pins out, using a garage press with a small amount of heat on the little end of the connecting rod, if they prove to be exceptionally difficult to shift, although overheating should be avoided at all cost; the metal can be taken to a blue colour but no more.

If the little end is accidentally overheated and turns red, it shows the temperature has reached at least 650°C, which can cause a strength reduction in the high tensile steel material from which the connecting rod has been made, and possibly result in a gudgeon pin coming loose, allowing it to go into the bore wall, subsequently ruining the engine. The same situation will be presented if there is an insufficient amount of interference fit retaining the gudgeon pin in the connecting rod. At the very least, each gudgeon pin and connecting rod little end must meet the minimum factory sizing requirements, but preferably be mid-way within the tolerance limit.

To ensure future reliability, all pre-used connecting rods should be Rockwell-hardness tested to ascertain the true status, as it is possible that, in the past, they may have been overheated and, because of this, become softer than when originally made, and therefore not up to standard. This entails testing the side of the connecting rod well away from the little end, to obtain a base line hardness value, before checking the little end and comparing the two; the values should be similar.

THE ESSENTIAL SOURCE BOOK

The vast majority of stock type automotive connecting rods are at least 25 Rockwell C, with aftermarket racing alternatives being in the vicinity of 35 Rockwell C. It is possible to re-heat treat stock-connecting rods to increase the hardness, with up to 30 Rockwell C being possible, which will increase their strength by roughly 7-10 per cent, but there will, however, be a reduction in durability. If it is deemed necessary, any heat treatment company can carry out this hardness testing work and re-heat treat connecting rods.

The re-heat treatment involves heating the connecting rod in controlled oven conditions to 850°C/1550F prior to quenching them vertically in oil. At this point, they will be approximately 50 Rockwell C, but brittle, and it is crucial to temper them back 25 Rockwell C to avoid failure, before being crack tested to verify they are flawless.

Following this, the little ends are checked for inside diameter size, and will usually be found on size, but if they are over-size, the connecting rod is considered a reject for a stock press fit gudgeon pin application. If, by this stage, the connecting rods are proved sound, they can then be shot-peened and have the big-end re-sized to the minimum stock tunnel bore size of 2.4362-2.4369in/61.880-61.987mm, which will result in 0.005-0.006in/0.127-0.152mm bearing crush.

The little end bores must be checked for size, as it is imperative they are within the stock range of 0.9104-0.9112in/23.124-23.149mm. If the bores are not parallel and to this size, then they are not reusable as press fit connecting rods, as it is impossible to remedy the fault, and a replacement will be necessary. However, they can be converted to a full-floating gudgeon pin arrangement, which involves honing the little end, making the pin a push fit into it, using Teflon or Aluminium buttons for its location.

When the crack testing issue has been resolved, all connecting rods should be straightness-tested by mounting the big-end of the connecting rod on a special jig, and checking the accuracy of the little end to it in two planes. The jig is capable of checking the alignment to within 0.0001in/0.0025mm.

As all these connecting rods are now fairly old, it is prudent to have the big-end ends re-sized after they have passed the alignment test. Engine re-conditioners clean up the matching faces of the cap and the connecting rod, by grinding 0.001-0.002in/0.0025-0.0508mm from each face. This reduces the big-end bore diameter in the longitudinal axis, before honing material from the big-end bore to bring it back to within the allowable tolerance size of 2.4362-2.4369in/61.88-61.987mm, with the smallest size being preferable.

CONNECTING ROD BOLTS

Although very robust, Cleveland engine stock-connecting rod bolts are knurled on the shanks to ensure a tight fit into the connecting rod, and this degree of tightness is an absolute requirement, as they are unserviceable if the bolts are not an interference fit into the connecting rod. However, technically, it is better if this is obtained without the knurling, as it can be the cause of stress points, which may eventually lead to a bolt failure. Though it can be said with certainty, there is no fault history attached to the stock Ford bolts. Aftermarket connecting rod bolt manufacturers make parallel shank bolts, designed specifically to be a very tight fit into the stock-connecting rods that are more desirable than the knurled components.

BLOCKING OFF THE PISTON SKIRT OILING SLOTS

An improvement can be made to the oil pressure before the connecting rods big-ends are re-sized.

The stock-connecting rods and bearing shell inserts have slots that allow piston skirt oiling. Eight connecting rods represent a considerable needless leakage factor in a racing engine, as there is already ample oil being sprayed around from the crankcase after leaving the bearings, which means it is possible to block off the piston skirt oiling, without detriment to lubrication.

This is achieved by 'Tig'-welding the edge of the cap, where the groove outlet is located. As experienced welders take only seconds to weld each cap, this procedure can be undertaken by applying a minimal amount of weld, without causing any heat distortion. The cap to connecting rod matching surface is then surface ground, to make it absolutely flat, as is the matching surface of the connecting rod, after the bolts have been removed; engine re-conditioners have special equipment to quickly and easily carry out this task, before new connecting rod bolts are fitted, and the connecting rod tunnel bore resized to the bottom factory tolerance diameters of 2.4362 to 2.4369in/61.880 to 61.987mm.

With each caps groove outlet welded shut, no jet of oil can pass out of the connecting rod via this means, leaving only the gap between the bearing and journal for the usual out-flow.

This procedure is also applicable and helpful when modifying connecting rods, as a means of preventing the big-end nipping up onto the crankshaft journal as listed directly below.

STOCK-CONNECTING RODS IN COMPETITIVE APPLICATIONS

In racing applications, the stock 351ci-2V and 351ci-4V connecting rods were often used during the 1970s in Cleveland engines. It was usual for two three or more to fail, with the remainder likely to follow suit, leading to the loss of the entire engine. This problem eventuated from the necessity to maintain an equal rpm performance with other comparable engines, and to attain this, it became necessary for them to be turned to 7000rpm. However, this proved impossible when equipped with these connecting rods, as, although not breaking in the first instance, the distortion in the connecting rod bearing tunnel was causing the big-ends to 'nip up' onto the crankshaft journal.

When the remaining connecting rods were inspected, it was clear to see that the big-end bearings across the bearing part-line, as opposed to 90 degrees to it, as perhaps expected, were scuffed on both sides, as metal to metal contact had occurred with the big-end journal, determining imminent failure.

This meant that, at high rpm, the connecting rod big-end tunnel bores were distorting, in turn reducing the connecting rod diameter across the bearing bore on the part-line. Initially, in an attempt to resolve this situation, the big-end bearings were given a minimum clearance of 0.0035in/0.088mm, which although reducing the amount of

PREPARING CLEVELAND V8 SHORT BLOCKS FOR RACING

contact between the surfaces of the bearing shells and crankshaft journals, did not stop the failures. An alternative solution was sought, as it is undesirable to use a huge amount of bearing to journal clearance, such as a minimum of 0.004in/0.20mm. The answer to the bearing problem was to build an amount of ovality into the big-end tunnel bore of the connecting rods, so that when the engine was turned to 7000rpm, although the tunnel bores distorted, they now became perfectly round, had the correct bearing clearance, and did not nip up on the crankshaft big-end journal. With this aspect resolved, they had a service life measured in hours before the 'I' beam broke. This can hardly be regarded as long-term reliability, but it was acceptable if an engine was only to be used for between 4 and 5 hours racing between rebuilds, after which time, the connecting rods were replaced.

The problem with the connecting rods, in this sense, lay with the 'strap cap' design, rather than if Ford had used a more rigid 'channel cap' or 'twin ribbed' design connecting rod cap. The strap caps are more flexible than channel caps, but allow cost savings in forging by way of the straight-shaped design, and are usually quite satisfactory for all normal road-going or rpm use up to approximately 6000. The stock production connecting rods cannot be considered faulty or as having a fault history, as they were not weak for their intended function, but simply had a limitation when used for purposes other than those for which they were designed. Although originally the problem was encountered on engines turned to 7000rpm, connecting rods intended for 6000rpm can be modified in this way, as a method of ensuring they do not nip up on the crankshaft. The stock-connecting rod tunnel bore diameter size is listed as between 2.4362-2.4369in/61.880-61.897mm.

To make the connecting rod big-ends oval, the eight connecting rods are crack and straightness tested, the small end diameter sizes checked to ensure correct interference fit for the gudgeon pin retention, and the part-line matching surfaces reground to remove approximately 0.002in/0.05mm from each, to guarantee they are all perfectly flat. The edges of the connecting rod and the caps are de-burred with a small needle file, before new connecting rod bolts are fitted. Two shims for each connecting rod are made the size of the cap footprint, from 0.003in/0.076mm steel or brass shim. These are then fitted over the connecting rod bolts, the caps fitted, the shims lined up with the connecting rod shape, and finally the nuts fitted and wound down, prior to being torqued to the fully recommended amount. Following this, the tunnel bores are resized to 2.4392in/61.956mm diameter, which is 0.003in/0.076mm larger than bottom factory size, after which the connecting rod nuts are undone, the shims removed, the cap and nuts refitted, the nuts torqued, and all tunnel bores checked for size. They should measure 2.4362in/61.956mm in the vertical plane or in-line with the 'I' beam of the connecting rod, and 2.4392in/61.9562mm if measured across the big-end tunnel bore inline, with the part line of the connecting rod/connecting rod cap. With all connecting rods measured and checked as being correct to this size, the next stage of the procedure is to check the 'bearing crush.'

All insert bearing shells require a certain amount of bearing crush, to guarantee they conform to the tunnel bore in which they are being 'held,' which, in the Cleveland engine, is 0.005in-0.006in/0.1270-0.1524mm. After machining the connecting rod tunnel bores with the 0.003in/0.076mm shims fitted, the tunnel bores should then measure 0.003in/0.076mm oval when assembled without the shims, and because of the oval making process, the 'crush height' needs to be checked and adjusted, as it may prove insufficient.

Bearing crush is checked by randomly fitting a pair of shells in any connecting rod, fitting the cap, and tightening the nuts to the required torque, loosening one connecting rod nut, and checking the size of the gap between the connecting rod, and the cap matching faces, under that particular bolt and nut. Although 0.005-0.006in/0.127-0.1524mm is requisite it could be slightly less, such as 0.002-0.003in/0.051-0.076mm, and the bearing crush will have to be increased by linishing (grinding) the cap to connecting rod matching surface.

It is necessary to be aware that bearing shells vary, and some re-mixing and re-matching between connecting rods can result in different bearing crush heights and diameter sizes, purely through this type of substitution. Although this can be a time-consuming process, it is absolutely essential for a racing engine.

Material is removed from the matching surface of the cap to reduce the big-end bearing bore diameter, in line with the connecting rod 'I' beam axis. Removing 0.001in/0.025mm from the cap will increase the feeler gauge measured bearing crush by approximately 0.003in/0.076mm, which although a very small amount of material, does, however, make a significant difference to the 'crush height.' Material is removed from the caps matching surface by hand linishing it across 220 grit wet and dry abrasive paper, atop a dead flat surface or, if preferred, using a surface grinder. When the bearing crush is restored to specification, the tunnel bore will almost certainly have approximately 0.003-0.004in/0.076-0.1143mm ovality.

When all the bearing shell inserts have been fitted into their respective connecting rods, and the amounts of bearing crush equalised, the bearing bores are measured in the vertical plane, in-line with the connecting rod 'I' beam, and each bearing bore and the crankshaft journals accurately measured to 4 decimal places. The connecting rods are paired for like sizes to the crankshaft journals, and to achieve the precise running clearances, the individual crankshaft journals may have to be micro-polished.

In most instances, they will all be the same, or within 0.0001-0.0002in/0.0025-0.0050mm, although it may be necessary to remark the connecting rods or list their paired order for fitting into the block. If needed, the crankshaft big-end bearing journals can be polished down to suit each pair of connecting rods for 0.003in/0.076mm clearance for a racing engine.

The objective is to remove equal amounts of material from each cap, making all the connecting rod big-end bores identically sized to four decimal places in the vertical and horizontal planes in relation to the part-line.

THE ESSENTIAL SOURCE BOOK

Further to this, the bearing crush height amounts need to be identical, and of a sufficient amount, and the bearing bores also to four decimal places or within 0.0001-0.0002in/0.0025-0.005mm/2.5-5.0 microns of each other. To achieve this aim, care and attention to detail is essential, however, it is a worthwhile task, as it is highly unlikely an engine will suffer a bearing failure through size discrepancy in the future.

A bearing clearance of 0.003in/0.076mm/75 microns is very acceptable, even if it is the upper level of the big-end bearing clearance allowance. The use of 50 weight mineral racing oil in the engine may be necessary to maintain sufficient hot oil pressure; a very suitable hot oil pressure for one of these engines is 70psi.

Note: 0.001in/0.025mm equates to 25 microns.

FITTING FOUR-BOLT MAIN CAPS ONTO TWO-BOLT BLOCKS

When alternative four-bolt caps are fitted onto a two-bolt block, the holes are 'spotted through' to the block, the caps removed, and the block clamped down onto a milling machine table or a radial drill, before being drilled and tapped. The main cap registers are the same for both blocks, and the material in the block casting is adequate to accommodate these two extra holes per main cap. After this, the main bearing tunnel bores have to be line-bored/line-honed, which means a small amount of material being removed from base of the caps, before they are bolted onto the block prior to being fitted and torqued to the correct amount. The main caps can be either aftermarket items or four-bolt main caps from a damaged four-bolt block. The main bearing tunnels are then either align-honed or align-bored to the bottom tolerance size of 2.9417in, which will ensure the main bearing shells have the maximum crush height.

OIL PUMP DRIVE SKEW GEAR

Throughout the years, many Cleveland V8 engines have failed skew gears for various reasons, with the most common being the surface finish of the teeth, as machined on the camshaft. The solution is to polish the camshaft skew gear teeth, using fine Emery tape, without distorting the shape of the tooth profile or reducing their size. This is a time-consuming and skilful process. The distributor drive skew gear is seldom at fault on the basis of surface finish, but they should be inspected and similarly polished if necessary.

The vertical height position of the distributor drive gear, in relation to the camshaft drive skew gear, is fixed by design, and, when assembled, should be precisely on the centre-line of the camshaft axis. It is always prudent to fit the camshaft and distributor into the block, and check the height position of the distributor drive gear, in relation to the camshaft skew gear. When the height size has been proven correct, the camshaft should be rotated, both clockwise and anti-clockwise, feeling for any 'grittiness' in the drive, which will be an indication of incorrect gear mesh or insufficient back-lash.

If any abnormality is discovered, the engine build cannot proceed until the matter is resolved because the drive is very likely to fail in the future, with the possibility of debris entering the engine via the oiling system, leading to potentially major damage.

It is absolutely essential to have sufficient back-lash of between 0.001 and 0.002in, with the two gears running smoothly against each other, especially in the direction of rotation.

An everyday driver Cleveland V8 engine in very original but well used condition.

Chapter 4
Camshafts

The original equipment camshafts for Cleveland engines covered a relatively wide range, from short to long duration (266-290 degrees), and the valve lifts from 0.427in/10.9mm to 0.491in/12.5mm. The engines were factory fitted, with both hydraulic and mechanical camshafts, but the vast majority were the former. The 302ci-2V, 351ci-2V, 351ci-4V, 351ciM-2V, 400ci-2V, and Cobra Jet 351ci-4V were all hydraulic while the 1971 Boss 351ci-4V and the 1972-1974 HO 351ci-4V engines used mechanical camshafts.

The 302ci-2V, 351ci-2V, 351ciM-2V, and 400ci-2V engines used hydraulic camshafts, with timing events in absolute terms of 256 degrees inlet, and 272 degrees exhaust duration, 0.422in inlet valve lift, and 0.427in exhaust valve lift. The intake valves opened at 17 degrees before top dead centre, closed at 59 degrees after bottom dead centre, the exhaust valves opened at 71 degrees before bottom dead centre, and closed at 21 degrees after top dead centre, giving a 34 degree overlap.

The 1970-1971 351ci-4V engines employed a hydraulic camshaft with timing events in absolute terms of 266 degrees of inlet, and 270 degrees of exhaust duration, and 0.427in lift on both valves. The intake valves opened at 14 degrees before top dead centre, closed at 72 degrees after bottom dead centre, the exhaust valves opened at 70 degrees before bottom dead centre, and closed at 20 degrees after top dead centre, giving a 34-degree overlap.

The 1971 Cobra Jet 351ci-4V engines used a hydraulic camshaft with timing events in absolute terms of 270 degrees of inlet and 290 degrees of exhaust duration, and 0.480in inlet valve lift, and 0.488in for the exhausts. The intake valves opened at 18 degrees before top dead centre, closed at 72 degrees after bottom dead centre, the exhaust valves opened 82 degrees before bottom dead centre, and closed at 28 degrees after top dead centre, with an overlap of 46 degrees.

The 1972 351ci-4V and Cobra Jet 351ci-4V engines used hydraulic camshafts with timing events, in absolute terms of 270 degrees of inlet, and 290 degrees of exhaust duration, and 0.480in of inlet valve lift, and 0.488in for the exhausts. The intake valves opened at 14 degrees before top dead centre, closed at 76 degrees after bottom dead centre, the exhaust valves opened 78 degrees before bottom dead centre, and closed at 32 degrees after top dead centre, giving an overlap of 46 degrees.

The 1971 Boss 351ci-4V engines used a mechanical camshaft with timing events in absolute terms of 270 degrees of inlet, and 290 degrees of exhaust duration, and 0.477in of inlet and exhaust valve lift. The intake valves opened at 34 degrees before top dead centre, closed at 76 degrees after bottom dead centre, the exhaust valves opened 86 degrees before bottom dead centre, and closed at 24 degrees after top dead centre, with an overlap of 58 degrees.

The 1972-1974 High Output 351ci-4V engines used a mechanical camshaft with timing events in absolute terms of 275 degrees of inlet and exhaust duration, and 0.491in inlet and exhaust valve lift. The intake valves opened at 17.5 degrees before top dead centre, closed at 77.5 degrees after bottom dead centre, the exhaust valves opened 77.5 degrees before bottom dead centre, and closed at 17.5 degrees after top dead centre, with an overlap of 35 degrees.

The valve lift of all of the mentioned camshafts, coupled with reasonable

39

THE ESSENTIAL SOURCE BOOK

valve spring rates, means good reliability and durability. However, such camshafts tend to have reduced valve lifts, compared to the aftermarket performance items, but for their intended purpose of powering road going car engines, they are generally very suitable.

In more recent times, Ford lists the M-6250-A341 hydraulic camshaft as suitable for high-performance applications, with their low-deck 351ci, and tall-deck 351ciM and 400ci engines. At 0.050in of lifter rise, the timing events cause the intake valves to open at zero degrees, before top dead centre, close at 34 degrees after bottom dead centre, the exhaust valves to open at 49 degrees before bottom dead centre, and close at 5 degrees after top dead centre, which is 214 degrees of duration for the inlet cycle, and 224 degrees for the exhaust. In absolute terms, the timing events are; intake opens at 39 degrees before top dead centre, closes at 73 degrees after bottom dead centre, the exhaust opens 83 degrees before bottom dead centre, and closes at 39 degrees after top dead centre, which is 292 degrees of duration for the inlet cycle, and 302 degrees for the exhaust, giving a 78-degree overlap. Inlet valve lift is 0.510in and the exhaust 0.536in.

Replacement part and aftermarket camshaft manufacturers are both good sources for these items, with all mainstream companies making a suitably wide range. Iskenderian, for example, offer several hydraulic camshafts for Cleveland engines starting with, in absolute degree terms, 262 degree through to 282 degree duration. The Iskenderian 262 Supercam has 0.488in valve lift, with the inlet valves opening 23 degrees before top dead centre and closing 59 degrees after bottom dead centre, and exhaust valves opening 59 degrees before bottom dead centre, and closing 23 degrees after top dead centre, giving a 46-degree overlap. Although these figures may appear very conservative in the eyes of many, they are ideal for a road-going engine. The 270 HL-HYD, a performance road-going camshaft suitable up to 6000rpm, has 0.510in valve lift. The inlet valves open 20 degrees before top dead centre, and close 70 degrees after bottom dead centre, and the exhausts open 64 degrees before bottom dead centre, and close 26 degrees after top dead centre, giving a 46 degree overlap. The 282 HYD has 0.516in valve lift, the inlet valve opens 33 degrees before top dead centre, and closes 69 degrees after bottom dead centre, and the exhaust valves open 69 degrees before bottom dead centre, and close 33 degrees after top dead centre, giving a 66-degree overlap. This component can be used in many racing applications, and is ideal for engines equipped with stock connecting rods turning no more than 6000-6200rpm. Iskenderian make excellent anti-pump-up hydraulic lifters to suit all their own hydraulic camshafts that can also be used with those made by other manufacturers.

High petrol/gasoline prices coupled with the requirement for fuel efficiency on the road, means that today, although many of the camshafts mentioned in this chapter are suitable for off-road racing applications, many are inappropriate for normal road use as for this function. Camshafts with low overlap figures of around 45 degrees are ideal, as are absolute durations in the vicinity of 260-270 degrees.

RE-GROUND CAMSHAFTS

Numerous regrinding companies can successfully restore a worn camshaft to an as new condition, provided that the lobes are all to specification hardness, effectively on size, and only showing signs of normal wear and tear. Only good, used camshafts can be reground, as a well worn camshaft lobe means a 'soft' lobe, and, as a consequence, the entire component becomes a write-off.

Many of these companies have the range, or partial range, of original factory profiles, which makes it quite possible to have the 1972-1974 Cobra Jet hydraulic camshaft profile ground onto a stock 351ci-2V or 351ci-4V item. It is not desirable to have more than this amount of valve lift, duration, and overlap for a road-going engine, as the miles per gallon will be detrimentally affected, irrespective of how carefully the car is driven. The camshaft fitted to any engine should always reflect the end use, as an over-cammed engine is rarely satisfactory, in spite of the impressive sounding idle.

A correctly re-ground camshaft is as good as new, and will usually last as long as the original. In the vicinity of 0.005-0.010in/0.125-0.25mm of material must be removed, to restore the camshaft lobes to their original specification shape. Grinding an alternative, non-factory, higher lift camshaft profile necessitates the removal of extra material from the lobes, particularly the base circle, which is acceptable, provided that the new amount of lift will not become substantially over 0.500in/12.7mm. New hydraulic lifters should be fitted to the engine, but if those used previously were nearly new, to restore them to an as new specification, they can be refaced by an engine reconditioner, using specialised equipment. Anti-pump-up lifters are required if rpm over 5000 is to be used.

All individual camshaft lobes are tapered as ground, to match the taper angle of the base of the lifter, but if the taper angle of the camshaft lobe has been incorrectly ground the opposite way, the lobe will fail prematurely, due to point contact with the lifter base. This compatibility is very simple to check by smearing each lobe with 'bearing blue,' inserting the lifter, rotating the camshaft one revolution, removing the lifter before inspecting, to determine whether its base has a covering of this substance from the centre to the edge of the lifter. If it has, this indicates full correct contact. Although incorrectly reground camshafts are rare, it does occur from time to time, but it only takes a few minutes to check all the lobes. As the first five-ten minutes of running a rebuilt engine are critical for both long-term camshaft durability and reliability, in order to avoid initial engine damage, it is paramount to always use a recognised break-in lubricant on the lifter bases and camshaft lobes. Ford, and all camshaft aftermarket manufacturers, make and list special break-in lubricants such as Ford's brand, M-19579-A12, or Wynn's 'Additif' or Gear Oil.

CLEVELAND FLAT TAPPET MECHANICAL RACING CAMSHAFTS

The mechanical high-rpm racing camshaft Ford offers within its wide range, with a reasonably broad torque band (part number M-6250-A342), is very popular. It has 43-73-84-42 timing, meaning the inlet valve opens 43 degrees before top dead centre, the inlet

CAMSHAFTS

valve closes 73 degrees after bottom dead centre, the exhaust opens 84 degrees before bottom dead centre, and closes 42 degrees after top dead centre. Absolute inlet duration is 296 degrees, while the exhaust is 306 degrees or 248 degrees of inlet duration, and 258 degrees of exhaust duration at 0.050in lifter rise. Valve lift is 0.580in for the inlets, and 0.606in for the exhausts, with 0.025in tappet clearances for the inlets and exhausts.

This camshaft can be used on racing engines, turning up to 7000rpm plus, and produces excellent power from approximately 3750rpm. Also, with few exceptions, it represents the maximum duration ever required for a Cleveland engine, although it has a fairly substantial overlap, which means the engine rpm should not be allowed to fall below 4000. Although camshafts with duration in excess of this are available from Ford and other companies, due to the loss of mid-range power, the Cleveland engine does not respond well to their use. Employing a camshaft with longer duration than the M-6250-A342 can possibly result in a slower car, because of its inefficiency at low rpm; therefore those with less duration can be beneficial. It should be noted that racing camshafts 'that work' between 3000 and 7000rpm will generally prove the most practical.

The aftermarket camshaft industry provides a wide range of suitable competition camshafts for the Cleveland V8 engine, with all being perfectly adequate for their intended purpose. Although there are several other examples, Iskenderians offer the FL-370 grind/part number 431370 mechanical camshaft, which is similar to the Ford M6250-A342 item, and has an advertised rpm range of 3000-7000, 0.528in valve lift, inlet opens 42 degrees before top dead centre, closes 78 degrees after bottom dead centre, exhaust opens 78 degrees before bottom dead centre, and closes 42 degrees after top dead centre.

ENGINE OILS

It should be noted that the ZDDP (zinc-dithiodialkyl-phosphate) is reduced/removed from modern engine oils to prevent contamination of catalytic converters, and increased emissions, and although this has had no affect on modern engines, it can seriously affect flat tappet camshaft small-block Ford V8 engines, all of which need to be lubricated with suitable ZDDP oils to reduce/eliminate the aspect of abnormal wear of camshaft lobes and lifter bases.

Valvoline makes three oils with a suitable amounts of ZDDP for small-block Ford V8 road-going engines, which offer sufficient protection; they are Valvoline 30W VR1-Racing, Valvoline 10W-30 VR1-Racing, part no VV-205, and Valvoline 20W-50 VR1-Racing. All these oils have a 1300 ZDDP rating, which equates to 1300 parts per million (ppm) of zinc, and 1200ppm of phosphorous. As other oil companies make similar products, it is advisable to check cross reference charts to find a suitable equivalent. The technical specification of any oil intended for use in a small-block Ford V8 should be checked to ensure the ZDDP is correct. Most oil companies have tech-lines, which can advise on the exact specifications of any of their products.

The standard oil for the Cleveland small-block Ford V8 engine was 10W-30, meaning it had a viscosity of 10 when cold, and 30 when hot. For warm climates where the temperature does not drop below around 40 F or 5°C, straight 30W oil or a 20W-50 can be used, but for climates where the temperature can be lower than this, 10W-30 is recommended.

351ci Cleveland V8 engine prepared for racing use in a four-door XY Falcon.

Chapter 5

Technical section

TORSIONAL VIBRATION

In the early 1950s, V8 engines were not factory fitted with torsional vibration dampers, as the engine power outputs versus the strength of the crankshaft were relatively low, and crankshaft displacement per cylinder firing was minimal, making crankshaft breakage negligible. At that time, most V8 engines had peak power outputs at less than 4000rpm, and would only have been tested at up to a maximum of 4250rpm on dynamometers used by the manufacturer, which showed few torsional problems at this engine speed versus the strength factor of the crankshaft. By the mid-1950s, sufficient numbers of engines were failing crankshafts during normal road use to warrant the US car makers to take note and rectify the situation, and when engines began turning higher rpm and generating higher power outputs, to guarantee crankshaft reliability, began incorporating crankshaft damping into engine designs.

From the late 1950s, most USA-made V8 engines were being factory fitted with elastomer-type crankshaft dampers 'tuned to 'respond' to the maximum amount of torsional displacement of the crankshaft' of the particular engine, which always occurred at the point of maximum torque. Most stock engines made during this period were turning a maximum of between 4000 and 4500rpm, with the maximum torque produced in the range of 2000-3000rpm. There was a high peak of torsional crankshaft displacement at 2000-3000rpm or maximum torque, which was the rpm range in which most stock engines were operating. Therefore, the crankshaft dampers were damping the largest amount of torsional displacement in the most frequently used rpm range, and as a result, few crankshaft durability problems were encountered with stock engines.

The typical elastomer damper has a maximum 'response' working range over a fairly narrow rpm band in the vicinity of 500-800rpm reducing as it rises above its recognised maximum efficiency point. This means that, in order to cover this peak, if an engine develops maximum torque at 2400rpm, the crankshaft damper will be designed to ensure a maximum efficiency range of between 2000 and 2800rpm. As the rpm rises above this, the stock damper still offers 'response' to torsional displacement, although on a diminishing basis.

Although the problem is termed 'torsional vibration,' that in reality, is not what is measured. While the engine runs on a dynamometer, a measurement is taken of the difference in the position of the front compared to the rear of the crankshaft; that is the twist in the crankshaft at the front, compared to the rear, which is the datum or reference point.

The engineering equipment employed to measure the positional difference between the front and the rear of the engine (known as carrying out a 'torsional survey') is called a 'torsograph,' and can be regarded as apparatus designed to be bolted on to and used in conjunction with any engine dynamometer. To ensure the engine rpm was precisely controlled, Ford always used an electric dynamometer for this type of testing.

The approximate 350lb armature of this machine acts like a very heavy flywheel, the rear of the crankshaft is therefore, directly connected to a component with a very stable constant rotational angular velocity. The torsograph weighs around 15lb or 6.5kg. The angular displacement between the front and rear of the crankshaft on a

TECHNICAL SECTION

constant basis has a reading on a dial of 0.14, 0.20, 0.24, 0.31 or 0.38 degrees upwards.

When an engine is at rest, the very front and rear of the crankshaft are in perfect alignment. A 'torsograph' has a fairly heavy supplementary flywheel-mounted 'pulse wheel' that, in conjunction with the original flywheel, gives a combined mass, which, when the engine is rotating, will ensure the rear of the crankshaft will be turning with constant velocity. A sensor able to measure a position on the 'pulse wheel' to within 0.001 degrees is set in relation to the 'torsograph' located at the very front of the engine, which has a similar measuring capability. The customary single retaining bolt employed to draw the crankshaft damper on to the crankshaft is used to retain the 'torsograph' in an angular position at the front of the crankshaft. When the engine is running, the 'torsograph' equipment and system is able to measure changes of angular velocity within a single revolution of the engine, by comparing the relative instantaneous positions of the front and rear of the crankshaft, the result being the torsional displacement between the two locations, or the twist in the crankshaft at any given rpm point, and loading on the engine.

A damper is purposely omitted from the engine when it is first tested, so as to discover the worst-case scenario of crankshaft torsional displacement. After a damper has been designed, made, and fitted, the engine will be re-tested, in order to determine the reduction and deflection in the crankshaft in a before and after test; the un-damped and damped conditions can then be compared for any improvement.

Further to this, the twist in the crankshaft is not constant in one direction, as it is continually varying around a mean amount, depending on the loading on the engine and the rpm at which it is turning. Every cylinder firing imposes an amount of twisting force into the crankshaft, therefore with every two revolutions, it receives eight combustion pressure load impacts. At each cylinder firing, the crankshaft is twisted in advance of the mean flywheel position, and when the force of that impact reduces, the crankshaft returns to its original position. However, in doing so, it goes back past that point through natural springing action, before coming forward to the mean position of the flywheel prior to the process being repeated, meaning the crankshaft is constantly subjected to varying degrees of both twisting and untwisting action.

Maximum engine torque occurs when the cylinder pressure peaks, and is a result of the engine achieving its optimum volumetric efficiency. The resultant crankshaft displacement is termed the 1st mode of torsional vibration.

Most stock engines, in road-going applications, use off-idle to the maximum torque potential much more than the maximum rpm capability, although many engines never see maximum rpm throughout their service life. As a prerequisite, engine manufacturers mostly design the crankshaft damper, so that it damps the torsional vibration or crankshaft deflection produced at maximum torque, before damping it above that and up to maximum rpm as a secondary consideration.

In the vast majority of instances, an engine would never exceed 0.50 degrees deflection un-damped, with only one or two engines ever showing above this amount when tested at Ford. The Ford Motor Company contracted crankshaft damper suppliers, including Schwitzer Inc and Simpson Industries, to make suitable dampers for particular engines, who then designed three or four to suit an engine application. They would then use the 'torsograph' test on the engine to find the most suitable, before supplying a mass-produced component for that specific model. The damper supplied would not necessarily be the same as used in another model of the same basic engine, such as a higher performance engine. A good example of this is the standard production 302ci engine damper, versus that employed in the Boss 302ci engines. Although the latter has very similar short assemblies, it produced more torque and bhp at higher rpm than the former; the dampers are designed to respond to these different values.

The objective is to have the 'outer ring' of the crankshaft damper turning at a constant speed precisely emulating that of the flywheel. The Ford Motor Company always works on the factor of having the crankshaft torsional deflection of any motor it made confined to within 0.25 degrees. Engines controlled within this amount are reliable and very seldom broke crankshafts.

In the early 1960s, when involved in making engines to run in the Indianapolis 500, Ford bought an Offenhauser engine to establish its power characteristics, and tested it very thoroughly at Dearborn. One of the tests involved checking the crankshaft deflection; these engines did not have a crankshaft damper. When the engine had been fitted with the torsograph equipment, it was fired up, and as it approached maximum torque, the torsional vibration became so severe that the torsograph, in a great sweeping action, was thrown off the front of the engine, hitting the wall of the building and was completely destroyed. Just prior to this unfortunate occurrence, the read-out was registering about 0.65 degrees, making it the highest Ford engineers had ever witnessed.

CARBURETTORS & INLET MANIFOLDS

Although very expensive during the 1970s and 1980s, four twin-barrel downdraught Weber or Dellorto carburettors were frequently fitted to Cleveland engines. Production stopped by both companies, but, in an effort to satisfy public demand, Weber (Spain) took the decision to re-make 48mm IDA carburettors, resulting in the current availability of brand new items. Secondhand inlet manifolds are accessible, as are new linkage systems. Although cost and availability means they are not often seen in use, this type of carburetion system is held in high regard, and for good reason.

Most enthusiasts fit Holley carburettors of varying Cubic Feet per Minute (CFM) sizes to these engines over all other types, although since its introduction, the Demon carburettor has made some in-roads into the Holley market share.

The two most commonly used inlet manifolds are the 180-degree dual plane and 360-degree single plane, with the former excellent for rpm from off-idle to 6000rpm, and the latter more appropriate for engines turning 5000 through to 7500rpm. However, provided that the camshaft duration and the carburettor

CFM are correct for the rpm range being used, either are adequate.

A camshaft with an advertised working range of between 2000 and 5500rpm will prove a good guide, but it should be noted that very often without too much trouble, engines with good cylinder heads, well calibrated ignition timing, and correctly sized and calibrated carburettors, will very often allow an engine to turn 500rpm more than expected. In the final analysis, fitting a longer duration camshaft can be a retrograde step, as it reduces the low rpm response and tractability. In the majority of instances, having an engine that pulls strongly from off-idle is the best option for most applications. As, on the whole, they vary little in cost, lower duration camshafts, such as 265-285 degrees, should always be considered for up to 6000rpm applications, as opposed to longer duration items which do not necessarily prove more efficient. Countless camshafts have been bought, only to be changed for an alternative with less duration before the engines became suitable for the designated purpose.

There has always been a tendency to 'over cam' engines, when in reality, the opposite is generally required. A little conservatism can pay dividends, because the engine will be more responsive at low rpm, which is often an area of the range used more than anticipated. Although long duration camshafts make an engine sound 'aggressive' at idle, unless the full advertised rpm range is actually being used, they are almost always inefficient, as the low rpm performance can be extremely poor and the mpg incredibly low. Vehicles in this condition are all too often unpleasant to drive, except for the odd time that the engine is higher within the rpm range.

Within the racing fraternity, there is little doubt that the 351ci 'low-deck' block engines fitted with USA-made 351ci-4V or Boss 351ci-4V 'quench' combustion chamber cylinder heads still remain the preferred choice. The 302ci-2V, 351ciM-2V, and the 400ci-2V engines are the least used in competition, but there is no reason why they cannot be modified to perform well in many applications.

Possible universal performance Holley carburettors suitable for use on Cleveland engines include the 350CFM and 500CFM two-barrel 2300-Series, 465CFM, 600CFM, 650CFM, 725CFM, 750CFM, and 780CFM four-barrel vacuum secondary 4160-Series, 600CFM, 650CFM, 700CFM, and 750CFM four-barrel mechanical secondary 4150-Series.

Using the basic Holley calculation for Cubic Feet per Minute (CFM) requirement, it can be seen that a reasonable range of two- and four-barrel carburettors can be employed. To calculate this, multiply half the cubic in size of the engine by the maximum rpm to be used, and divide the answer by 1728, before multiplying this number by the efficiency rating of the engine. The answer reached will give the CFM required for the engine.

The efficiency rating is the variable, often leading to a slightly larger than necessary carburettor being fitted, resulting in an unnecessary loss in low-rpm performance.

The tendency is to over-estimate the efficiency rating of the engine, but the following guide should prove helpful; for all intents and purposes, a stock engine is approximately 75 per cent efficient, a medium modified engine 85 per cent, and a racing engine 95 per cent. It is important, however, to realise that this is only a basic guide and not an infallible rule.

A smaller CFM carburettor may possibly provide better low-end rpm response, and very similar top-end performance, while a large carburettor might only give optimum top-end power, and be somewhat inefficient in comparison practically everywhere else within the rpm range.

Experimentation is often the only way to determine the merits or drawbacks of each combination on an individual engine. A good rule is not to use a four-barrel carburettor until the CFM rating of a two-barrel has been exceeded. Many engines have proved to perform equally well with a two- as with a four-barrel Holley, and, on occasion, not as well! The extra complexity over the basic simplicity of the two-barrel is almost universally seen as essential to obtain the highest possible performance level, but this is not totally correct for all circumstances – simplicity is often the best policy.

302ci engines

Efficiency	Engine	rpm	CFM req
75 per cent	302ci	5000	327
85 per cent	302ci	6000	445
95 per cent	302ci	7000	581

The 350CFM and 500CFM two-barrel 2300-Series Holley carburettors, and the 465-600CFM four-barrel 4150 or 4160 Holley carburettor, can easily accommodate the 302ci engine.

351ci engines

Efficiency	Engine	rpm	CFM req
75 per cent	351ci	5000	381
85 per cent	351ci	6000	445
95 per cent	351ci	7000	675

These results show the 500CFM two-barrel 2300-Series Holley carburettor and 465CFM, through 700CFM four-barrel 4150 or 4160-Series Holley carburettors, can accommodate the 351ci engine airflow requirements.

400ci engines

Efficiency	Engine	rpm	CFM req
75 per cent	400ci	5000	434
85 per cent	400ci	5500	541
95 per cent	400ci	6000	590

These figures illustrate that the 500CFM two-barrel 2300-Series Holley carburettor and 600CFM four-barrel 4150 or 4160-Series Holley carburettors can accommodate the 400ci engine airflow requirements. It is never ideal to fit a very large carburettor to an engine, unless it is to be constantly turning at 5000rpm and above, and since they are not difficult to change, various types can easily be tried to establish the differences in efficiency. Holley carburettors are readily available, with many enthusiasts having access to at least three or four through friends and associates, allowing them to try a range of CFM carburettors, and decide upon the best suited for an individual application. Using the calculation will find your particular starting point carburettor.

It is paramount to use a good air filter, and although many types are available, the 14in round component is the most popular, with the dropped down base-type giving the lowest overall height. To prevent any dirt passing between the surfaces, it is always advisable to seal the air filter element to the air-cleaner base and top, using a

TECHNICAL SECTION

silicone sealer. The filters are inexpensive and are of low restriction.

INLET MANIFOLD OPTIONS

Several inlet manifold arrangements are available for the Cleveland engine. Firstly, there are the factory cast iron, dual plane inlet items, which are reasonably efficient, and should not be regarded as being poor examples, and replacement presumed the best course of action.

Although weight is the perceived problem, often leading to them being changed for lighter aluminium counterparts, they work adequately up to 5000rpm, and are certainly very acceptable as starting point inlet manifolds – not too much work is involved in changing one to try another type.

While the available range of inlet manifolds for Cleveland engines is adequate, it is not as wide as that of other USA-made V8 engines. The low-deck are more extensively covered than the tall-deck engines. Edelbrock make one inlet manifold appropriate for both 351ciM and 400ci engines, listed as a 'Performer 400,' which has now superseded all other 180-degree dual plane types. First developed in the early 1960s by Buick, it was used on its large capacity engines because of its equal inlet tract length design. Ford also employed this configuration in 1968 on its 428ci big-block engines, and in the same year, Chevrolet also used it in its Z28 small-block engines.

Based on the cylinder head inlet port sizes, Edelbrock have divided low-deck Cleveland engines into two groups. The 'small port' 302ci and 351ci engines use an Edelbrock 'Performer 351-2V' inlet manifold, while the 'large port' 351ci engines use the Edelbrock 'Performer 351-4V,' both of which follow the same basic runner configuration, and are excellent to 6000-6500rpm.

Edelbrock make two further inlet manifolds for large port, cast iron cylinder heads, low-deck Cleveland engines, the 360-degree single plane or 'spider' type known as 'Torker 351' and 'Victor Series.' The 'Torker 351' has a lower rise than the Victor Series, and offers better under bonnet/hood clearance. The very popular 'Torker 351' is suitable for 7000rpm operation plus, and is an ideal 360-degree single plane inlet manifold, allowing rpm to the point of maximum cylinder head airflow at 7000rpm. If the installation can stand the height requirement, it can be considered far the best choice for racing applications up to this level.

FUEL

In order to utilise the optimum amount of ignition timing and air fuel ratio, allowing for the development of maximum torque and brake horse power, it is requisite to match the engine compression ratio to the fuel being used. Failure to do this results in poor engine performance, and possible engine failure, through piston and probable connecting rod damage.

Building more compression into an engine than the fuel can tolerate is pointless, as the use of over rich mixtures, and retarded ignition timing necessary to prevent combustion problems, significantly reduce engine output.

It is essential that an engine being used in a racing application has a wide-open throttle acceleration capability, as anything less will prove detrimental.

Having to reduce the amount of throttle to prevent pinking, or worse detonation, is far from ideal; over-compressed engines are definitely inefficient.

Fuels are rated using Research Octane Number/RON and Motor Octane Number/MON systems. In the late 1920s, the USA-based Co-operative Fuels Research Council devised a fuel sample test to determine the octane ratings of gasoline mixes, resulting in the development of a very special single-cylinder engine, with a variable compression ratio and ignition timing, which has become commonly referred to as a CFR engine. The same engine is used to test fuel samples, using two different test procedures. Prior to a fuel sample being tested, the CFR engine is calibrated, using a pure chemical reference mixture guaranteed to be 100 octane before it is run in the engine. The RON method of obtaining a rating necessitates the CFR engine to be run at 600rpm, with a set amount of ignition timing, as prescribed by ASTM D2699/IP237, which is 13 degrees ignition timing before top dead centre. This is regarded as being representative of the fuel capability both for starting and idle purposes. American Society for Testing and Materials (ASTM) and D2699 is the criteria of the RON test. The Institute of Petroleum (IP) has 237 as is its number for the same test.

The MON method of obtaining an octane rating is conducted using ASTM 2700/IP236. The CFR engine, in this instance, is run at 900rpm, the compression ratio increased, and the ignition timing advanced while the engine is running. The octane rating derived is representative of how the particular fuel sample will cause an engine to run on the road, under both cruise and motorway conditions. The MON is more significant, for evaluating the fuel suitability, than the RON octane rating system, even though this is the most widely advertised at pumps world wide. For example, there are 91 RON/83 MON, 94 RON/84 MON, 96 RON/86 MON, 97 RON/87 MON, 98 RON/88 MON, 98.1 RON/87.5 MON, 99 RON/87 MON, and 102 RON/90 MON.

While still using the RON and MON tests, the USA introduced an additional system, enabling buyers to purchase the fuel best suited to their needs, which was the anti-knock index number (AKI), based on the RON and MON added together and halved. Other names for this system are PP (Pump Posted) or PON (Pump Octane Number). When discussing octane ratings, the testing criterion needs to be clearly understood.

Although the majority attempt to keep with the cheaper brands, motoring enthusiasts in the USA have the choice of an extensive range of fuels for off-road applications. Specialist fuel companies including VP, F&L Racing Fuels, Sunoco, and Sports Racing Gas, market a range of high octane leaded and unleaded fuels, although their products are more expensive than fuel available at the pumps. This is to be expected, as they are re-refining or reprocessing the fuel they buy in from bulk suppliers. Sunoco GT100 unleaded street-legal fuel is advertised as being 100 octane, but is essentially 105 RON and 95 MON, making it excellent for high compression engines. Sunoco also make an off-road 109 RON and 99 MON unleaded fuel, named GT Plus, equivalent to Sunoco GT100, VP C10, and VP Motorsport 103. Sunoco makes 'Standard Leaded' for racing purposes, which has 115

THE ESSENTIAL SOURCE BOOK

RON and 105 MON octane ratings, containing 0.99g of tetraethyl lead per litre. Sunoco 'Supreme Leaded' has 114 RON and 110 MON octane ratings, with a 1.12g content of tetraethyl lead per litre. Sunoco 'Maximum Leaded' has 118 RON and 115 MON, and contains 1.32g of tetraethyl lead per litre. VP and Sports Racing Gas make equivalents. Avgas in comparison is 107 RON and 100 MON, with 0.8g of tetraethyl lead per litre.

As a general rule, engines with 8.3-8.5:1 compression will require 91 RON and 83 MON octane rated fuel, 8.5-8.9:1 compression require 94 RON and 84 MON octane ratings, and 8.9-9.5:1 compression 97 RON and 87 MON. The street-legal Sunoco GT100, with octane ratings of 105 RON and 95 MON and Avgas, will support 11.0:1 compression in these engines.

To achieve good running, it is essential to run the correct air/fuel mixture ratio, usually approximately 12.3-12.5:1, which produces the optimum torque and bhp throughout the rpm range. The ideal amount of total ignition timing, with a quench type combustion chamber, is in the region of 36-38 degrees. The requirement for the ability to use the correct/ideal amount of total ignition timing is that the compression ratio must match the octane rating of the fuel.

The optimum air/fuel ratio is found by testing the fuelling on an engine or rolling road dynamometer, or on a track, in conjunction with scientific analytical equipment connected to the engine. With general fuelling built into the engine, it is tested for torque and brake horse power, while at the same time monitoring the exhaust temperatures, ensuring they do not exceed 750°C/1550F. The mixture is made progressively richer in small steps, until the torque and brake horse power readings begin reducing, through the mixture becoming too rich. At this point, the mixture is slowly made leaner to find the point just before the torque and brake horse power begin reducing, through it becoming too lean; the middle position is the optimum. When this procedure has been completed, the engine is subsequently tested in its working environment at the race track. To guarantee they measure up to or surpass previous engines, prior to fitting engines into cars, numerous race teams run them on an engine dynamometer and 'drive'

them on a rolling road, before taking them to a track to be tested against known data. Engine operating temperatures, air-fuel ratios/Lambda readings, and ignition timing amounts are all carefully monitored throughout this procedure. With the advent of data logging equipment, Lambda readings are constantly being taken, displayed, and recorded, and can be monitored by the driver, and later downloaded to be scrutinised by mechanics, in order to check the air/fuel ratios levels during a race.

ENGINE COOLING

Although frequently lacking in many Cleveland engine installations, engine cooling is a critical issue. Large amounts of money are often spent on engines and practically nothing on radiators, ducting or hose pipe work, making an excellent engine appear mediocre for some very simple reasons.

The ideal running temperature for these engines is around 70°C/160F, with the plus and minus amounts being 65-75°C/150-170F.

If, during a racing event, the engine temperature rises above 80°C/180F, the engine will begin to lose power, and the higher the increase, the greater the power loss. Frequently, this factor can be checked through lap times, because the car's speed decreases as the race progresses. There are obviously other reasons for temperature increases, including being behind another car for any length of time, and not having undisturbed air passing through the radiator core, but it is clear that as this rise occurs, the vehicle will definitely become slower. The solution is to ensure the vehicle is fitted with an efficient cooling system, capable of maintaining the coolant temperature at a nominal 70°C/170F, with only the slightest possibility of it ever exceeding 80°C/180F.

Numerous Cleveland V8 engine-powered cars suffer cooling problems, and the inefficiencies of the system are usually clearly visible the instant the bonnet/hood is opened.

During a race in the 1990s, a Cleveland-powered Mustang was observed by the author performing well, although it failed to win. At the start of the race, the car pulled away at great speed, immediately taking the lead, leaving the rest of the field behind

and seeming unlikely to catch up. Two laps in, it was still well ahead, but on the third appeared slower, with the other cars behind rapidly closing the gap. Next time around, it had already been overtaken once, and on the sixth lap, two cars had passed. Nearing the end of the race, the car was running fourth, but not performing as it had when the engine was cooler. When the race finished, the car pulled into the pits with steam wafting through the grille, and, having switched off the engine, the driver got out and went to the front of the car to open the hood. Inspection of the instrument panel revealed the needle was off the clock on the temperature gauge, meaning it was showing something in the order of 120°C/250F plus. When the hood had been lifted to allow cool air to circulate around the engine, the basic problem with the car became apparent, as there was an old vertical flow radiator with a number of repair patches, and steam was leaking from several areas. Further to this, there was insufficient air being fed to the radiator core via the standard arrangement. A discussion with the driver revealed that he had no idea of the problems he was encountering, because he thought, as this was a racing car, the high temperature registering on the gauge and the steam emanating from the grille and hood area of the car after a race was normal.

This car needed a large crossflow aluminium radiator divided off into sections, to enable the coolant to flow in the air stream at least twice, if not three times, before returning to the engine.

In this case, the air should have been ducted from behind the grille to the entire radiator core, which would have involved some slight alteration to the original bodywork and aluminium ducting fabrication, to force the maximum possible volume of air to pass through the core, as the air passing through the radiator core is drawn downwards underneath the car, creating the necessary through flow.

The stock water pump was being turned to around 8000-8500rpm, when it should have been geared to turn between 4500-4750rpm or an absolute maximum of 5000rpm. The high looping top radiator hose employed had no place on such an engine, as this type of top

TECHNICAL SECTION

hose is a potential air trap, and can be the cause of poor coolant circulation.

The engine bay scene, on the basis of coolant temperature management, was unbelievable, yet it is a common problem, even though the information to prevent these situations occurring has been available for many years.

Preparation for good cooling capability

When rebuilding an engine, it is essential to remove all the accumulated sediment that can collect in the coolant passageways through years of use. The block and cylinder heads should always be placed in a 'hot tank' cleaning system, containing an alkaline mix of a water-based caustic soda solution. The tank is heated to between 60-90°C/140-195F. The higher the temperature within this range the better, and parts can be left soaking overnight. All core plugs need to be removed, and the camshaft bearings protected, if they are not being, or have recently been, replaced. The cleaner the coolant passage ways and the closer to bare metal, the better, and all engine reconditioners have specialised cleaning equipment at their disposal to carry out this inexpensive procedure.

It is strongly recommended to use an anti-freeze solution as a means of keeping the internal passage-ways of the block and the cylinder heads clean.

Radiators

When fitting a radiator, the maximum possible amount of the core should be exposed to the air stream, although the side tanks of a crossflow radiator are less important, and do not need to be directly in the air stream. As the aftermarket industry now produce a wide range of crossflow aluminium radiator sizes, very large items have become available for any size installation at a reasonable cost.

The top radiator hose should always be in the same plane as the top radiator inlet, or if possible, inclined slightly from the outlet on the engine to the top of a side tank. All hose pipe work should have smooth flowing curves devoid of restriction, although curving around objects is acceptable. The fitting of a low 90-degree turn, custom-made water outlet onto one of these engines is often essential to meet this requirement.

The radiator can have the filler cap fitted into the top of one of the header tanks, but if this is done, it needs to be on the opposite side to the inlet pipe from the engine to the radiator.

Header tank cooling systems

In many instances on modern engines, a header tank system is used, and although it works well, to ensure maximum efficiency, there are aspects that need to be checked. The system works on the principle of the reservoir/header tank/expansion tank being the highest part of the cooling system, and the contained coolant offers an amount of 'head' on the basis of keeping the entire engine full of coolant. Consequently, the coolant level is kept constant in the engine, while the level of the header tank will vary slightly during the engine operation cycle, with the coolant contained always feeding down from the bottom of it into the return pipe, going from the bottom of the radiator to the primary side of the water pump.

Strategically placed small diameter pipes in the cooling system feed any air bubbles formed up into the air gap of the header tank, effectively expelling them from the coolant being circulated through the engine. These pipes sometimes need 1/16in diameter hole restrictions positioned in them to limit possible coolant flow when an engine is turning high rpm; the objective is air bubble removal, and not coolant flow bypass.

The hot coolant needs to pass through the radiator core, and not be bypassed back into the engine at near maximum temperature, as can happen if too much is allowed to circulate in this way.

Coolant reservoirs/header tanks/expansion tanks can contain in the vicinity of ½ gallon with ⅓ of the total volume of the header tank an air gap.

Water pump and alternator speeds

Racing cars are not normally fitted with thermostats, however, road cars need one to ensure rapid warm up. In most instances, all that is needed to gain the improved coolant circulation necessary for racing applications is to remove the thermostat, and make sure the water pump is turned at a suitable speed, but no faster than necessary, to obtain an ideal coolant temperature of around 70-75°C. Many stock engine water pumps turn at crankshaft speed, although some are faster. Careful consideration should be given to the water pump drive pulleys, to ensure the water pump speed does not exceed 5000rpm at maximum engine speed.

The stock-pressed steel vane water pump impellor, with straight vanes, is efficient to a maximum of 5000rpm, before the onset of cavitation, and therefore turning the water pump to a maximum of between 4500-5000rpm on a racing engine is very acceptable. Turning the water pump at the lowest possible speed conducive to optimum coolant circulation is a necessary requirement, as this will reduce the power loss to drive the water pump to a minimum. If a water pump is turned too slowly, an engine will begin overheating at low rpm, but will start to run cooler the instant the engine is turned to higher rpm. This is because water pumps need to be turned to a certain speed to become efficient, and to be geared accordingly by using various sized drive pulleys.

High performance engine water pumps are equipped with reverse involute vane impellors, and can be turned to 7000rpm and maintain pumping efficiency without cavitation. However, these also need to be geared correctly, as no water pump should be turned faster than necessary.

Alternators usually cut in and begin generating power at around 900-1000rpm, which means if an engine idles at 1000rpm, the alternator also needs to be turning at roughly the same speed. As a general rule, stock alternator pulleys are far too small for racing engines, and need to be changed for larger ones approximately the same size as the crankshaft drive pulley. In order to ascertain whether it is putting out a minimum of 13.8v to a maximum of 14.4v, after installation, the alternator must always be carefully checked and regularly monitored for any current output loss.

ENGINE TUNE UP

Cleveland engines were all made during the period when two- and four-barrel carburettors and distributor type ignition systems were employed. It is

47

THE ESSENTIAL SOURCE BOOK

not impossible to convert them to have electronically controlled ignition and fuel-injection, but it is costly compared to fitting up-rated original equipment items. In the main, enthusiasts tend to remain with carburettors and distributor ignition systems. Rebuilding/retuning Ford original equipment fitted carburettors can be challenging in some instances, but substituting the original with a Holley for a performance application removes any problems, while in turn allowing for substantial power gains.

As a means of ensuring maximum efficiency throughout the rpm range, all existing and rebuilt engines need to have the ignition timing tailored to the engine's state of tune, and the octane rating and type of fuel to be used, and the carburettor set up for ideal mixtures under all load conditions. These two aspects of engine tuning go hand in hand, and provided it has been rebuilt correctly, there is no reason whatsoever why any Cleveland engine cannot be adjusted to give extremely good power, coupled with optimum fuel economy.

When these engines were first introduced for the 1970 car model year, only leaded fuel was available, followed by the addition of low-lead fuel in 1971, and unleaded in 1975, which remains the only current petrol/gasoline in the Western World, and therefore used in the vast majority of Cleveland engines.

In the first instance, unless only low mileage is predicted, and the engine never used under excessive loading, where excessive heat is generated (as they preclude the incidence of valve seat recession), fitting hardened exhaust valve seats is a necessity. Alternatively, a fuel additive can be used for the same purpose. Although costly, these measures will solve the problem or potential problem. The requirement is to guarantee all the exhaust valve seats are fitted correctly, with the correct amount of interference fit in the cylinder heads, which is 0.004-0.005in, with the valve seats shrunk-fit into the cylinder head by freezing the valve seat inserts, and warming the cylinder head. This guarantees the prescribed interference fit, in turn ensuring there is no possibility of them dropping out while in service.

Over the years, stock Cleveland V8 engine ignition timings have ranged from 4-8 degrees to around 8-12 degrees before top dead centre (BTDC) static ignition timing, at an idle speed of 750-1250rpm, to 34-38 degrees BTDC of total ignition timing, at between 2750-3750rpm, with roughly 10-15 degrees of vacuum advance.

To avoid internal engine damage, due to lean mixtures during full power tests, the air/fuel ratio needs to be set at 12.3:1-12.5:1, to obtain maximum power, although a slight reduction may be possible. It is imperative to scrutinise the readings throughout the initial testing, to guard against lean mixtures, and ensure the ratio is kept at the prescribed level. These engines can be expected to tolerate idle speed mixtures in the region of 14.7:1-15.0:1, and a cruising speed mixture of 15.5:1-15.75:1. As the aftermarket car industry make reasonably priced quick acting air/fuel ratio meters for fitting into cars, this can be easily monitored on a permanent basis.

Matching the RON and MON octane ratings of the fuel to be used to the engine, and specifically the compression ratio, is paramount, as if the compression ratio is too high, it is impossible to set the ignition timing correctly for optimum burning rate. Setting the ignition timing retarded, to avoid pinking under acceleration loading or any loading is a futile exercise; it is preferable for the compression ratio to be reduced.

There are some variations in the rates and amounts of ignition timing in the range of standard distributors, therefore it would be quite wrong to assume that any Cleveland distributor is suitable, as the individual requirements have to be found by testing, and those settings are then built in. Some Ford-made distributors will have the correct internal components, including 10 and 11-degree cam-plates, which simply entails thoroughly cleaning the distributor before fitting two ideal advance mechanism springs, and renewing all other components. The Mallory Dual Point distributors excel in this application, as, provided that all relevant parts are at hand, they are adjustable on the basis of rate and amount within minutes, offering optimum power and fuel economy. Huge amounts of power and fuel efficiency can be lost if the ignition system is not set correctly for a specific engine, therefore far from being a minor aspect of engine tuning, it is vital that the distributor/ignition system is optimised.

Initially, any Cleveland V8 engine could be set with four to six degrees of static ignition timing, and 32-34 degrees of total ignition timing, which is 28 crankshaft degrees or 14 distributor degrees of mechanical ignition timing advance built into the distributor, with the rate of advance set, enabling the total ignition timing to be achieved at between 3250-3750rpm. Although all Cleveland engines will run successfully with these settings, they can be refined in order to achieve optimum engine performance throughout the rpm range.

Depending upon the engine build, fuel, and application, the maximum ignition timing settings can be considered as 16-18 degrees BTDC, at an idle speed of approximately 1250rpm, the total ignition timing of 36-38 degrees BTDC, as soon as 2750-3000rpm is reached; these are maximum amounts and should not be exceeded.

Using accurate crankshaft damper markings, a stroboscope timing light, and in-car air/fuel ratio monitoring, it is quite possible to find the optimum ignition timing settings. Further testing allows small adjustments to be made to both the ignition timing and carburettor, to make the jetting richer or leaner as appropriate. The vacuum advance canister can be changed for an alternative that allows the maximum possible amount of ignition timing, such as between 10-15 degrees under cruise/load conditions. This fine tuning is very time-consuming, but once achieved, the car and engine combination will deliver optimum driveability, using the minimum possible fuel.

When tuning an engine, the objective is to maintain the ignition timing at the highest possible level within the listed range, without pinking during acceleration or under load, simultaneously ensuring the air/fuel mixture remains at an adequate ratio level in all situations. This prevents the engine surging, due to it either being too lean or causing excessive fuel consumption, owing to being too rich.

Enthusiasts will find the following books from the same author helpful in achieving optimum results/engine performance:

TECHNICAL SECTION

How to Build & Power Tune Distributor-Type Ignition Systems
How to Power Tune Holley Carburettors
How to Choose Camshafts & Time Them for Maximum Power

PARTS

Although, for some years, used 4V and Boss 351ci cylinder heads and four-bolt blocks have not been readily obtainable, all necessary parts including pistons, rings, main, big-end and camshaft bearings, valves, valve springs, valve spring retainers, split locks, camshafts, lifters, gaskets, rockers, and related components, are accessible from the aftermarket and replacement parts industry. The only unavailable new Ford-made items are blocks, cylinder heads, crankshafts, and connecting rods, but sufficient numbers of these core parts remain in circulation, enabling enthusiasts to build a Cleveland engine.

EMISSIONS

Although car industries were constantly looking at new ideas to improve their engines, there is little doubt that without the legislation introduced in 1966 in the State of California, they would not have developed the necessary technology to meet the requisite emission levels as quickly, and of their own volition. In many instances, the technology to attain the levels was non-existent, but the awareness of the need to improve the situation hastened the progression. A prime example of this evolution is electronic fuel-injection, which ultimately transformed the way an internal combustion engine could be run on the basis of efficiency, however, this was not introduced until 1978. Ford had begun working on mechanical fuel-injection in 1958 under principal design engineer Paul Brown of Advanced Engines, but it was not until the mid-1960s when Ford began to look at Bendix electronic fuel-injection, that the situation began developing rapidly. Bosch was then, and still remains, the world leader in electronic fuel-injection technology, and after subsequently switching to the use of to these components, Ford had EFI engines on test in its laboratories by the mid-1970s.

The first automotive emission control was instituted in 1962, when cars sold in the State of California were required to replace the road draft tube arrangement with positive crankcase ventilation, to prevent engine fumes entering the atmosphere.

Los Angeles is the largest city in the world built on a desert area, with hills to the north and east, and these factors combine to hold a range of pollutants, until certain weather conditions prevail. The California Air Resource Board (CARB) considered cars were totally responsible for all air pollutants, and in 1964, decreed that from 1966, as a means of reducing these levels, it would become mandatory for all new cars to be fitted with emission controls that reduced the hydro-carbons by 72 per cent, carbon monoxide by 56 per cent, and a total elimination of crankcase fumes. Carbon monoxide (CO) is caused by incomplete combustion, and hydro-carbons (HC) are partially burnt particles of fuel in the atmosphere.

In a 'free combustion' environment, over time, a domestic bonfire will burn until only ashes remain, which is quite unlike an engine where the air/fuel mix burns in a 'controlled combustion' environment, where there is insufficient time to complete the burning process. This results in the residual mixture exhausting from each cylinder every time the exhaust valves open, which produces carbon monoxide and hydro-carbons.

The California Resource Board did not enter into discussions with the automobile manufacturers in the mid-1960s, as to the best overall strategy to tackle the problem, but simply dictated the way forward, as it was adamant in its belief that cars were the prime reason for air pollution; had it been correct in its assumptions, the air would have become cleaner in Los Angeles much more rapidly.

When government environmental agencies began investigations into industrial pollution and demanding solutions to the problem, levels reduced significantly in some of the worst affected areas, which is not to say the authorities were incorrect in their actions to force automobile manufacturers to fit emission control equipment, but it certainly proved cars were not the only contributor to the problems. Car manufacturers were an easy target, as undoubtedly the 100,000,000 plus cars on the US roads, with numerous poorly tuned big engines, were causing excessive pollution.

As a result of these initial actions, car engines in the countries that have adopted emission controls are absolutely clean, and, ironically, generally far cleaner than the industries making many of the components for the vehicles.

At the time, car manufacturers stated quite categorically that, although the suggestions were acceptable, the overall solution to the problem needed not only the availability of high-octane fuel, but also 'lean burn' engines specifically designed for its use. In the first instance, time was needed to develop both a higher refined fuel and suitable engines. The overall objective from the perspective of the car manufacturers was to obtain the maximum energy from a gallon of fuel, while simultaneously generating the least emissions, before dealing with the exhaust gases. However, their suggestions and requests for adequate time to carry out these measures were largely ignored, and as a result, it took many years to reach the current state of affairs. This could possibly have been achieved in half the time, and saved vast amounts of fuel and unnecessary exhaust gas pollution, as the amount of fuel burnt, to achieve the lower level of pollution aims, was vast.

To control carbon monoxide and hydro-carbon pollution, engines were fitted with Thermactor or 'air injection' systems, which comprised of an engine driven vane compressor or 'smog pump' with the air it compressed, then injected into the exhaust manifolds. Here, the contained oxygen caused further exhaust gas burning as a 'post combustion' or 'after-burning' process within the exhaust system, prior to being emitted into the atmosphere. However, this after-burning process caused the exhaust systems to run at higher temperatures, with the cast iron exhaust manifold becoming dull red under certain load conditions, and there were a few occasions when the under car exhaust pipes came into contact with long grass, setting it alight! Although this type of emission control remained in use for many years, its operation eventually became far more sophisticated.

The necessary pipe work, the cost

THE ESSENTIAL SOURCE BOOK

and maintenance of the smog pump, together with the fact that on the basis of rich and lean mixtures, it was a little hit and miss due to the inaccurate carburettor metering, meant that, although the air injection system worked, it was not entirely satisfactory. This type of emission control system was used as the primary method of hydro-carbon and carbon monoxide emission limitation, until the 1975 car model year.

Announced in 1966, and starting in 1968, the Federal US Government decreed that all cars sold nation-wide were to have emission controls fitted, and these types of systems were then installed into all North American cars. It was mandatory for all cars to comply with the Federal Test Procedures (FTP), which involved checking the CO percentage and Hydro Carbon gram levels of the exhaust gas emissions from the system, at an idle speed of approximately 1500rpm, and at 2500rpm, with the engine under no loading. To be successful, test results had to prove the levels to be below a specified amount. Once again, the agencies dictated their demands to automobile manufacturers without discussing an overall strategy first.

In 1970, the US Congress passed the 'Clean Air Act,' and established the Environmental Protection Agency (EPA), and, as a result, in 1970, 'low lead' content fuel was introduced. Up until this time, fuel could have up to a maximum of 4.0g of tetraethyl lead per US gallon for the high-octane fuels available, even though around 2.5g was typical. Tetraethyl lead was seen as a major health hazard, and fuel companies were instructed to reduce the level of lead in fuel to 0.5g per gallon, which was the amount thought by the EPA to be sufficient to prevent valve seat recession. This occurs when engines with 'soft' exhaust valve seats designed to run with leaded fuel are used with low lead fuel with an insufficient tetraethyl lead content, and the cast iron cylinder heads erode when in contact with the exhaust valves, as was the case between 1970 and 1974. The valve seat recession from standard could be massive, such as $3/16$in, and engines stopped once the hydraulic lifter internal mechanism had bottomed out, and they were unable to compensate for the valve movement back into the cylinder head; the exhaust valve was then held away from the eroded valve seat.

After discussing the reduction level, engineers from various major car manufacturers, who had become very concerned about the outcome of this new legislation because of the imminent damage to most existing and forthcoming new engines, collectively told the EPA, before the fuel was introduced, that this would not be adequate for all engines, but that 1 gram in the fuel would likely offer sufficient protection for all engines in a good serviceable condition, which would still be a huge initial reduction in tetraethyl lead. The government and the FPA would not consider 1 gram, and as a result, thousands of otherwise good engines failed exhaust valve seats, resulting in large unexpected bills for millions of car owners, with an increase in pollution and fuel consumption, while these engines were failing. Few people at the time fully understood the changes to the fuel and the probable devastating effects to their engines over time. When car owners, facing huge garage bills, approached the car companies with regard to some form of compensation, they were often very disappointed with the negative response received. If the cars were under warranty, they were entitled to some recompense, but if the vehicle was older, they were simply informed that the new fuel was a government initiative, and not the manufacturers' responsibility. Either way, these unnecessary costs to both the general public and the car industry ran into millions of dollars.

Starting from 1970, the US Government required all emission control equipment to carry a warranty for 5 years or 50,000 miles.

In the early 1970s, shortly after becoming aware of the compulsory introduction of un-leaded fuel for 1975, as a means preventing valve seat recession, Ford began testing V8 engines equipped with induction-hardened exhaust valve seats, using the well known Torcco process; proven successful, this process was universally implemented in all new 1975 model year car engines.

Tetraethyl lead boosted the fuel octane rating at low cost, which allowed car manufacturers to use high compression ratios, making the engines as efficient as possible, and lubricated the exhaust valves and valve seats.

The subsequent loss of the tetraethyl lead meant a reduction in compression ratio, engine efficiency, and the use of retarded ignition timing, which resulted overall in much higher fuel usage. So while emission levels were reduced by approximately 50 per cent, the miles per gallon usage increased markedly, by roughly 25 per cent in many instances, which to a large extent nullified the entire measure. Although, without a doubt, the lead content in the air began reducing slightly, because it was not only car emissions that were the type considered as environmentally unfriendly, the overall impact of the measure was minimal.

Oxides of nitrogen are deadly poisonous gases formed when nitrogen and oxygen are subjected to high temperatures such as 2700F, and, as a measure to reduce levels for 1972, cars were fitted with Exhaust Gas Recirculation (EGR) systems, which could return an amount of the exhaust gases back into the engine. Oxides of nitrogen could not form when the peak combustion temperature was lowered, through the recirculation of approximately 10 per cent of the exhaust gases back into the engine via the inlet manifold exhaust-heat cross-over passageway. Initially, a vacuum operated valve mechanism was employed, and later a vacuum and engine temperature operated component; the system did not operate at idle speed. EGR reduces peak power outputs by reducing the intake charge density.

As they did not comply with the current emission regulations, some new Ford cars were unsaleable, and for 1973, it was necessary for them to be re-certified, which was achieved by retarding the ignition timings by roughly 4 degrees. With retarded ignition timing, engines run hotter in the combustion chamber, which, in turn, leads to higher exhaust temperatures, a better after-burn and less emission. However, the drawback to this adjustment is the loss of power and increased fuel consumption, as, on average, engines lose 2-3mpg, but at this time, as it was mandatory for the engines to be re-certified, there was no alternative. The

TECHNICAL SECTION

engineers were only able to use this method of reducing emissions as fuel economy was not included in the official requirements, but it was not a means they would normally have chosen.

'Dura-Spark' electronic ignition systems were fitted to all Ford V8 engines for the 1974 car model year, to replace the distributor points with a maintenance free system that did not necessitate regular replacement, and ensured the spark integrity under all conditions over a very long period.

Catalytic converters could only be employed using unleaded fuel, which first became available in North America from July 1974, just prior to the release of 1975 model year cars on October 1 that year, and saw the introduction of these efficient and simple devices that reduce the toxicity of exhaust gases through a chemical reaction. All new North American cast iron V8 engines then featured either induction-hardened exhaust valve seats or pressed in-hardened exhaust valve seat inserts, to prevent valve seat recession due to the lack of lubrication previously offered by tetraethyl lead.

The very first catalytic converters used the precious metal platinum to oxidise the carbon monoxide to carbon dioxide, and the un-burnt hydrocarbons to carbon dioxide and water, to comply with the current requirements. As platinum was very expensive, palladium and platinum were then used in combination but platinum was eventually phased out, when the cheaper palladium was proven to be almost as satisfactory and adequate to meet the requirements.

In 1975, the Evaporative Test Procedure was established, which involved a new car, without the engine running, being placed in a sealed room, and the subsequent collection and analysis of evaporative emissions from the entire vehicle, including those from the rubber, paint, glass, metal, plastic, and carpet. At this time, this practice applied only to cars, whereas literally thousands of manufactured mechanical products would have fallen into this category.

The Government-initiated Constant Volume Sampling (CVS) began in 1975, with the aim of reducing car exhaust emissions by 75 per cent. The procedure entailed collecting all the exhaust gases pumped into an enormous bag over approximately 15 minutes, while the car was under test with the engine set to simulate a general driving pattern over 20-25 miles; the sum total of the emissions collected was categorised and the test assigned a number constituting a pass or fail. All cars had to go through this procedure annually, but after using millions of gallons of fuel to conduct these tests, this system became unviable and was finally abandoned.

Ford introduced the solid state Electronic Engine Control system (EEC) on some V8-powered 1978 model year cars, which, apart from the distributor spindle and the crankshaft, had no moving parts. The ignition timing signal was taken from a four-pole pulse ring, positioned at the rear of the crankshaft, with a sensor located in the rear of the block, and the distributor was for high-tension current distribution only. This system remained in use until the end of the 1979 car model year, when it was replaced in 1980 by EEC II and EEC III in 1981, both of which varied from EEC I in that, as a simplification measure, the crankshaft position sensing was re-located to the front of the engine on the timing chain cover.

The Cleveland V8s were only ever factory fitted with two- and four-barrel carburettors, which, in an effort to achieve a more consistent mixture control of air and fuel for the various loading and operating conditions, became more complicated in the 1970s through to the early 1980s. However, by the mid-1970s, it had become very clear to automotive engineers that the carburettor was outmoded, and the way forward lay with electronic fuel-injection and electronic ignition, controlled by engine management systems. All Ford V8 engines used carburettors, until a number of 1982 model year cars had the first of the electronic fuel-injection systems fitted.

By various means, from the mid-1960s to the mid-1990s, car exhaust gas emission levels in North America were reduced by approximately 90 per cent. In certain areas of some cities in the USA, for example, it was proven from random sample tests that the atmospheric air going into engines was dirtier than that emitted from the exhaust pipes of cars fitted with the latest pollution control equipment; the cars were, in fact, technically cleaning the air.

Currently, there is much controversy regarding car exhaust emissions, and the distance covered per gallon, as fuel consumption varies greatly depending on the weight, the streamlining, and engine efficiency of the vehicle. Today, a small European car with a 1.5-litre, four-cylinder engine might cover 100,000 miles, averaging approximately 35 miles to a US gallon, equating to a total of roughly 2900 US gallons, which would require 65 x 44-gallon oil drums. A two-litre, four-cylinder engine-powered car covering 100,000 miles, averaging 25 miles to a US gallon, equates to around a total use of 4000 US gallons, or 90 x 44-gallon oil drums. In days gone by, a USA-made, medium-sized car with a 5.0-litre V8 engine would cover 100,000 miles, averaging about 15mpg, amounting to roughly 6600 US gallons, and this would fill 150 x 44-gallon oil drums. However, 250 drums of this capacity were needed to power a large 7.0-litre V8 engine car, averaging 9 miles per US gallon over 100,000 miles, using a staggering 11,000 US gallons.

Measures for reductions in car emissions still receive high priority in the Western World, which seems ludicrous, when such little apparent regard is given to the industrial emissions produced, when manufacturing colossal numbers of vehicles per annum, that easily outweigh those from automobiles. There is no accurate data regarding industrial versus car emissions to make a true comparison, but it is quite probable that, during its service life, a 1960s car might equal the pollution levels created during its manufacture, whereas modern cars are now somewhat cleaner and therefore produce less toxic gases.

Currently in North America and Western Europe, the car industries and finished products are environmentally clean, although huge sums of money are still being invested into making them even cleaner, for what amounts to a very small percentage of the total World pollution, while many other countries have no emission controls whatsoever on either automobiles or industrial waste. Air pollution is a global issue, but many countries with high concentrations of industrial areas, although prepared to manufacture components relevant to these problems, do not require their cars or industries to comply with any emission or pollution regulations.

Western world environmental agencies are currently demanding more fuel efficient cars, necessitating the implementation of leaner air/fuel mixtures, which will involve a complete move away from the less economical Lambda 1 or 14.7:1 air/fuel ratio-focused engine management systems, to those that can operate with 13.0:1-60.0:1 air/fuel ratios, while not emitting noxious gases. This requirement will entail new designs, including un-throttled direct injection engines, with the rpm controlled by the ignition timing, and the amount of fuel injected, in turn, necessitating further massive investments from automobile manufacturers.

To keep and correctly maintain a car over several years is a much greener option than changing it after only a short while, as this simply increases the demand for new vehicles. Car manufacture is basically controlled by demand, therefore the lower this becomes, fewer will be made, which, in turn, leads to reduced industrial pollution.

Often, due to expenses incurred for a seemingly simple repair, numerous, perfectly good cars are scrapped well before necessary, as a high percentage of the public are reluctant to pay large sums of money fixing an old car, instead preferring to invest in a newer model, which can lead to further pollution problems associated with the energy used in the recycling processes.

Even when fuel was very inexpensive, engine manufacturers always gave great consideration to the importance of its economy within the framework of their current technology, but the governmental agencies seemed not to connect this aspect with the subsequent car emissions. The ideal goal would have been to extract the maximum energy from the fuel, with the minimum amount of emissions, which is what engine manufacturers told the environmental agencies from the beginning, but unfortunately, their advice fell on deaf ears.

As cars had to sell at affordable prices, automotive engineers worked to meet the emission requirements at the cheapest possible rate, and employed innovative ideas to keep their costs as low as possible. An improved component may only have cost an extra $5 per engine, however, its overall development by a team of engineers could have cost up to $5,000,000, and may only have remained in production for a few years, before needing further modification to suit a new requirement. Costing focused on the price per item only, rather than the sum total of both the item and its development, and as the cars had to remain competitively priced, the cost of the latter was difficult for auto-manufacturers to recover.

In summary, the car emission situation could have been tackled successfully, in the late 1960s or early 1970s, if the environmentalists had taken the time to listen to the advice of the engineers. Although the governmental agencies were correct in facing the increase in air pollution, had they united with the automobile industry and entered into serious discussions, accepted their suggestions with both sides agreeing on one overall strategy, the whole matter could have been resolved more quickly and easily, and at less expense for all concerned, together with colossal fuel savings.

Chapter 6

Cleveland V8 racing history in NASCAR & Pro-Stock

In 1969, when NASCAR announced the transition from 426ci, 427ci, 428ci, and 429ci or 7-litre, big-block V8 engines, to 366ci small-blocks, to take effect in 1972, to comply with the regulations, Ford took the decision to produce a Cleveland engine of this capacity for the 1971 Boss Mustang to become known as the 'Boss 366.' Although the Mustang car was not used in NASCAR racing, this presented no problem to the racing authorities, as they merely required Ford to make sufficient numbers of a particular engine to be fitted into Ford cars to satisfy the homologation rules. In the event, NASCAR allowed Ford to enlarge the stock 351ci engine to this capacity limit, without the need to make a production run of 366ci engines, and as an alternative, the 1971 Boss Mustang was fitted with a 351ci engine. The earlier special Boss 429ci engine, for example, had been made, and fitted into Mustang cars, purely to homologate the engine for NASCAR racing. The Ford Fairlane-based Talledaga cars were never factory fitted with the Boss 429ci engine, although they were installed by NASCAR teams, solely for racing applications.

As a means of using existing engine technology, Ford engineers de-stroked the 620bhp 429ci big-block NASCAR engine to 366ci, but, when tested, it gave 475bhp, which was 50bhp down on the development small-block 366ci NASCAR Cleveland engines that had been developed simultaneously, thereby enabling an evaluation of both engines.

In 1969, the 427ci FE 'side-oiler' engines were successfully employed in the aerodynamically-designed Talledaga car for the early Super-Speedway events, until the 429ci NASCAR engine became available, and subsequently used for the remainder of the season, seeing winning places in all events, apart from the race at the Talledaga track late in the year, when high speed tyre wear problems led to all major teams boycotting the event.

When it became obvious to Ford engineers that the stock 351ci Cleveland cylinder block was incapable of taking the 0.080in over-bore necessary to make it 366ci, in July 1969, approximately fifty special Boss 366ci Cleveland blocks were made at CEP1, coded SK-46362. These dry-deck blocks were designed to have a uniform minimum 0.200in wall thickness after being bored to 4.080in. The necessity to make a special block for racing purposes was no reflection on the original stock item, as this had been designed for passenger cars with a smaller bore than requisite for NASCAR applications. As long as an item met all durability requirements, Ford avoided using any excess material in stock castings.

When Ford engineers re-worked the stock block to obtain the 0.080in over-bore capability, in order to achieve the 366ci capacity, they simultaneously investigated measures to improve its overall strength. This was finally attained by thickening the three centre main bearing webs, to reinforce this area of the block, while the front and rear webbing was only altered on the inside of the crankcase to maintain the stock external appearance. Although, outwardly, they were visually the same, they varied internally from the stock production block, and were made from Ford's AC grade cast iron, with an additional 5 per cent nickel specially formulated for racing engine blocks, which dramatically increased the strength over the stock component. The main caps were larger than Boss 351 items, and made from SAE-D5506 specification nodular iron. The 366 Cleveland NASCAR block weighed

THE ESSENTIAL SOURCE BOOK

approximately 190lb, which was roughly 20lb heavier than the stock production item, weighing around 170lb.

SK46250 became D0AE 6015-H, used for first series RX-452 engine builds.
SK48417 was used for second series RX-452 engine builds.
SK46363 became OSA XE-152118, and finally C9ZE-6015-D/revison M.
SK6877 and SK48419 were both dry-deck block.
SK50271 – 366 block with ribbed iron main caps.
SK42617 – alloy Indianapolis block.
Other blocks were; SK46372, SK46380, SK4612, SK50332, SK50294, SK46382, SK56841, and SK56747.

All of the above blocks were made before the move from EEE Engine Engineering to the Kar Kraft building, before March 1970, and all were 366ci/4.080in bore capable.

The cylinder bores were siamesed to within approximately 2in of the bottom of the water jacket, which meant there were no coolant passageways between the bores at the top, and coolant was only able to circulate between the lower part of each bore, and around the two end bores per bank of cylinders. These special blocks were always referred to as '366' blocks, and not Boss 366 blocks as originally intended.

To qualify for the Ford durability test, the 366ci NASCAR engines endured a minimum of six hours at full throttle and maximum load, with the engine turning between 6500 and 7500rpm. By the end of 1970, an engine had achieved this without failure, but it became necessary for the second and fourth main bearings to be run with 0.004in/0.10mm bearing clearance.

Two of these engines were fitted in Talledaga cars, one a Holman-Moody, driven by David Pearson, and the other a Jack Bowser, driven by AJ Foyt, and tested at the Ontario Speedway in late 1970, but following a noticeable rise in water temperature at around 30 laps, both engines failed the Boss 302ci type Reintz cylinder head gaskets. The head gaskets were obviously insufficiently robust, but as no alternatives were available, they were changed immediately once they had failed, and the test programme was completed under these conditions, clearly proving a better head gasket was needed. Between October 1969 and January 1970, the Special Engines Group moved from Electrical and Engine Engineering to Car Product Development, based in the Kar Kraft building on Haggarty Road, East Dearborn, where the Cleveland racing engine development continued, and all newly developed and subsequent components were given the code prefix XH, as opposed to the SK or XE of Engine Engineering.

On 19 November 1970, Ford Vice President Matthew McLaughlin made a statement declaring that Ford was reducing its racing activities, apart from some limited divisional and dealer support for some Pro-Stock drag and off-road racers. The 'Special Engines Development' section of the 'Special Vehicles Department' of the 'Product Development Office' vacated the Kar Kraft building and relocated to California, where the 351ci Cleveland racing engine development continued for Pro-Stock drag racing. The Special Engine Development shipped all components to a workshop owned by Bill Stroppe in Long Beach, California, where his engine builders subsequently assembled the engines, and, as no racing engine testing was allowed at Ford in Detroit, following its decision to quit car racing, transported them the short distance to the Autolite dynamometer facility. Here, under the direction of Art Chrisman, they were run and tested on a Heenan-Froude water brake dynamometer. Ford had previously completed durability tests on all various components at its dynamometer test centre on Oakwood Boulevard opposite the EEE building, therefore any further trials carried out in California were purely to determine the amount of achievable power available for Pro-Stock drag racing. The peak power reading shown on a dynamometer during the first half of 1971 was in the region of 550-575bhp, at approximately 7500rpm. Primarily, this work was undertaken to assist Don Nicholson, who had acquired some support funding from Ford Division, at the stage when the 366 blocks had a 4.000in bore, as opposed to 4.080in, and were not dry-decked, but designed to work in conjunction with the new McCord five-fold, flame-ring type head gasket.

As soon as the new McCord head gaskets were perfected in early 1971, the dry-deck blocks were no longer used, as not only did it involve a complicated procedure to fit the cylinder heads, the blocks were extraordinarily expensive to machine, and the relevant gasket sets very costly. The dry-deck blocks worked perfectly; even if a sealing ring began to leak during a race, only that particular cylinder would be affected, and the combustion pressure would leak to atmosphere, and not into the cooling system, causing it to pressurise, and, in turn, leading to engine failure. Ford switched from the dry-deck block sealing system, mainly as a means of making its racing engines more similar to its high-performance road-going engines.

In November 1970, when Ford quit the racing scene, well over a year of work had been invested in the 366 cylinder block, however, as racing would continue without its presence, Ford Division unofficially made funds available for the 'Special Engines Group' to assist both Pro-Stock and NASCAR racers. Therefore, albeit from the sidelines, Ford remained involved within the sport. In 1971, Don Nicholson used the first 366 block in his Pinto for Pro-Stock racing, with a 4.000in bore, as opposed to 4.080in normally employed in NASCAR engines. Although listed as a Boss 351ci, which with this specific bore size was correct, in reality, the block Ford supplied was a NASCAR 366.

During the 1972 NASCAR events, when using a Talledaga fitted with the 366ci Cleveland engine, Bud Moore encountered problems not previously discovered during dynamometer testing at Ford: an approximate 3in vertical crack randomly appeared on the thrust side of a bore wall of the block, which, as the offending cylinder pressurised the cooling system, caused the engine to lose all the coolant. To rectify this problem, Ford engineers strengthened the bores by altering the water jacket cores, so that when the blocks were cast, they had 'square bores,' where the coolant flowed around the cylinders. Each bore wall then became a minimum 0.280in thick in four places, which, without compromising the coolant flow through the block, was considered the maximum width possible.

Ford made special heavy-duty

CLEVELAND V8 RACING HISTORY IN NASCAR & PRO-STOCK

connecting rods for NASCAR racing, coded XH-10385 and XH-10827, but, due to cap failures, the early version was problematic. However, this was rectified and the later items, while being quite heavy, proved almost failsafe. All these connecting rods were tested safe to 8000rpm, which meant they had been tested on Ford's Stroker machine, the apparatus employed to test connecting rod durability to 8500rpm. This machine cycled a connecting rod, simulating the peak loads in compression and those under tension, providing very accurate performance capability data. They were initially used in NASCAR by Bud Moore Engineering in 1972, however, as the race authorities approved the use of aftermarket components when the supply of Ford factory items was depleted, he changed to the lighter Carrillo 'H' beam.

Originally Kellogg-manufactured, Ford supplied forged crankshafts marked XH-19847, although some later crankshafts were made by Atlas. Apart from a 0.080in larger diameter, the special XH-10588-marked forged pistons made for this engine by TRW were the same basic design as those used in 1969 and 1970, in the Boss 302ci Trans-Am racing engines.

Originally, a maximum of roughly 150 SK and 50 XH prefix coded special Ford NASCAR-type blocks were cast, but with an approximate 20 per cent scrap rate due to casting flaws, engine durability testing, bore size trials, other development purposes, and supplies for Pro-Stock drag racing, few were left available for NASCAR. Most of the early blocks had been made applicable to the expensive dry-deck system but when the much cheaper McCord head gasket system became perfected they were no longer used. Throughout 1972, and until 1975, Bud Moore successfully employed Ford NASCAR blocks, carrying either the SK or XH prefix casting code, with other racers also using them when obtainable in 1974-1975.

As the cylinder heads employed during 1972 were identical to the 1970 Boss 302 Trans-Am items, many of the first engines built used the earlier components. Boss 302ci Trans-Am cylinder heads and Boss 351ci Cleveland heads were interchangeable on both Boss 302ci racing engines and Cleveland NASCAR engines, as the water outlets were positioned on the front face of the cylinder heads, going directly to the top of the radiator, and not into the inlet manifold or block, before going to the radiator. To make the 366ci Cleveland engines more competitive, NASCAR gave Ford racers a dispensation, allowing them to alter the cylinder heads, which involved milling the cylinder head casting, and doweling and bolting an aluminium plate with differently machined shaped ports, which raised the exit angle of all the exhaust ports. The port 'roof' and 'floor' angles were altered and raised by about 45 degrees.

Although this procedure was carried out in 1971 by Don Nicholson, and in 1972 at Bud Moore Engineering, originally, the idea had been conceived in late 1969, when the Ford 'Race Group' was still in the Engine and Foundry Division. An investigation began into the prospect of using the Boss 302ci engine in the Indianapolis 500, and the decision was taken to manufacture both 302ci and 351ci versions, using aluminium blocks and cylinder heads to reduce them to a minimum weight. Although roughly 20-25 sets of components were made and fully machined during August and September, 1969, no engines were ever assembled or tested.

Having spent many years at GM, working specifically with matters pertaining to the small block Chevrolet V8 engine, Smokey Yunick had current knowledge in this field, enabling him to make accurate comparisons between cylinder heads. When he followed William Knudsen from GM to Ford, he was asked to give his valued opinion on a pair of the new aluminium Boss 302ci Indianapolis racing programme cylinder heads. In October, with full permission to make any changes he deemed necessary, he took a pair to his workshop in Daytona, before returning them after approximately three months, having altered the exhaust ports by welding the floor and topside of the cylinder head casting. This allowed the exhaust port exit to be raised by approximately 1in from its original position, thereby lessening the acuteness of the turn. As he considered the inlet ports flowed excessively for a 302ci engine, he also put forward the recommendation that they be made smaller, which confirmed earlier conclusions reached by Ford engineers, and this aspect was changed on the 1970 Boss 302ci Mustang. However, as it would have entailed a major external casting change, and be illegal under Trans-Am regulations, the exhaust ports were not altered to his specifications, although the overall power improvement, through raising the exhaust ports, was noted by Ford engine engineering.

When it became the intention to use the Cleveland engine for Pro-Stock in 1971, although the basic cylinder head casting could not be changed, Ford engineer Robert Wendland, who worked within the Special Engines Group, thought out the idea of machining the cylinder heads away on the exhaust side, and fitting plates. This would enable the exhaust ports to be raised, implementing the criteria devised by Smokey Yunick, to obtain the power gain. As he originally felt aluminium would be incapable of withstanding exhaust heat of 700-800°C/1300-1450F, the first three or four pairs of plates made were cast iron. However, his ensuing testing with aluminium plates proved they were perfectly satisfactory, and finally became the chosen material. When Ford first fitted them to its Hilborn-fuel injected 366ci test engine, the outcome was very encouraging, as it developed 595-597bhp – an increase of 20bhp over the best result with the original Boss 302ci Trans-Am cylinder heads.

This technology was shown to Bud Moore Engineering, and Gapp & Roush, who both used the system very successfully. Although Bud Moore retained the original Ford square port configuration, Gapp & Roush developed a round exhaust port, while using the same basic system.

In 1972, Bud Moore Engineering used stainless steel racing inlet valves, as made by Eaton for the 1970 Trans-Am Boss 302ci racing programme in the 366ci NASCAR engines, and employing the original valves was a logical extension of that usage. At this time, Ford engineers were developing Titanium valves in conjunction with TRW. However, they encountered a problem, as, to prevent the top becoming 'mushroomed' over in use, either hardened tips on the top of the valve stems or a lash cap was needed.

THE ESSENTIAL SOURCE BOOK

Although it took time to perfect the 'inertia welding' of a Stellite tip onto the top the valve stem, it was eventually achieved by TRW. Titanium valves were subsequently very successfully used in NASCAR racing, from late 1972 onwards, with the inlet valve weight usefully reduced from 105g to 85g. Although Bud Moore eventually used these valves, initially he was not overly keen to try them, as he had concerns about possible failures. The Eaton stainless steel hollow-stemmed exhaust valves, weighing 95g, from the 1969 and 1970 Boss 302ci Trans-Am series, were retained.

The 366ci engines were fitted with a special XH-10693 crankshaft damper made by Simpson Industries, with response values to suit high rpm operation, which although looked similar, was wider than the Boss 302ci Trans-Am racing engine counterpart. As much as possible, the crankshaft was internally balanced, which in reality meant there was in the order of 15oz/in of external balance on the crankshaft damper hub and the flywheel, much the same as used on the Boss 302ci Trans-Am engine.

During later dynamometer testing, the Ford Engineers decided to try the crankshaft damper used on the Boss 302ci TransAm racing engines. This crankshaft damper, which descended from the 1968 'Tunnel Port' 302ci Trans-Am engine, proved to be most suitable for these engines, as it removed a serious valve train harmonic. With this positive result, all remaining used examples were rounded up at Ford, and sent to Bud Moore Engineering and the Woods Brothers, for use on their NASCAR engines. Ford eventually had them remade by Simpson, and sold them under Part Number M-6316-A3, as listed in its SVO catalogue. This part is still available today.

Bud Moore Engineering was the only entrant using the 366ci Cleveland V8 engine in NASCAR racing in 1972 and 1973, and while his cars performed very well with unrestricted induction, they were not quite as fast as the restricted induction 7-litre, big-block engine-powered cars. This was not necessarily a reflection on the power output of the new engine, as there were a few problems which affected engine reliability, but overall, he gained a great deal of success with this engine.

At the end of 1973, a letter was issued by the Vice President of Ford, Phil Benton, demanding the immediate cessation of all race activities, which meant there would be no further assistance whatsoever from the company, or its personnel, for the racers.

358CI NASCAR ENGINES 1974

When the Boss 351ci Cleveland engines first became available, Red Farmer, who was sponsored by Ford, began using them for oval track racing. Although performing very well, cylinder bores began to crack during events, and always in the same place in the bores. After three or four engines had failed through this problem, Red Farmer turned to Venolia pistons for advice on solving the issue. Specifically for his use, they made several sets of 360-degree fully skirted items, which spread the loading across the thrust side cylinder wall, unlike the TRW pistons, which concentrated it over a small area. He also encountered a second problem with cylinder head gasket failure on the inlet port side. The solution was to 'post' the cylinder head under each inlet port, to support the head gasket surface more satisfactorily. A hole was drilled and tapped in the head gasket surface, a stud wound in and tensioned against the underside of the inlet port, the stud cut off, and the cylinder head gasket surfaced. Red Farmer's Cleveland engines then became reliable, and he went on to win numerous races in fields where he was often the only Ford entrant.

The NASCAR engine capacity was reduced to 358ci for 1974, as the Chevrolet V8 engine block could not be altered for a 4.080in bore, while maintaining sufficient strength for racing purposes. Therefore, essentially, the 366 by 4.080in bore blocks were obsolete, and new blocks with 4.030in bores were required.

When, in 1974, Red Farmer first began driving for Wood Brothers Racing, the company was employing the regular Boss 351ci four-bolt main cap block, bored 0.030in oversize. This brought it to the required 358ci capacity, and not the 366 NASCAR block with Ford-recommended TRW 'slipper skirt' pistons. At his first race meeting with this company, he asked Leonard Wood which pistons he was using. On receiving his reply, he told him that so equipped, it was pointless even starting the engine, let alone racing it, as without doubt, from his experience, a cylinder wall would fail during the race, and consequently they did not enter the event. As Leonard Wood regarded Red Farmer as one of the best stock car racers of all time, he readily heeded his advice, and after fitting the one remaining set of alternative 'full skirt' Venolia pistons Red Farmer was able to provide, he won the next race. From this point, this particular company supplied Leonard Wood with the same components.

HEAD GASKETS

As a means of making its racing engines less specialised, and more in line with the stock production items, Ford took the decision to switch from the dry-deck block principle, and began using the stock Boss 302ci engine Reintz head gaskets. However, as these could not maintain the compression seal, and leaked on the inlet manifold side of the engine, in an attempt to prevent head gasket failure, Ford fitted screw-in posts from the top of the cylinder head, down to the back of each combustion chamber, to make it less prone to distortion, and achieve improved support for the cylinder head gasket matching deck surface. Although the posting system enhanced the reliability to a limited degree, the improvement was minimal, and not considered a cure for the problem. Cylinder heads were then cast with integrated post supports, but because they could not be tensioned against the back of the combustion chamber, they proved less successful than the screw-in posts, and Ford subsequently asked McCord to initiate a new special gasket specifically for racing applications. He devised a 'five-fold' sealing ring head gasket, which completely eliminated the compression leakage problem.

As it had previously proved to be of some help towards head gasket reliability, screw-in posting remained in use, until the change to the all-new aluminium cylinder heads in the early 1980s.

CLEVELAND V8 RACING HISTORY IN NASCAR & PRO-STOCK

ALUMINIUM CYLINDER HEADS, 1982

During the late 1970s, Chevrolet, Pontiac, Oldsmobile, Buick, and Ford were competing in NASCAR racing, with all these GM cars using the all cast iron, 350ci, small-block Chevrolet engine. GM was the driving force behind the change from cast iron to aluminium cylinder heads, as, on the basis of adding material by welding, they were easier to both modify and repair.

By 1980, Ford's stock of production and replacement part Boss 351ci Cleveland cast iron cylinder heads – used by the NASCAR racers – were running low, which necessitated making additional reserves. To be reliable in racing applications, these cylinder heads were both posted and made to have high exhaust ports, which involved considerable reworking and expense. However, an agreement was reached between all the various teams, that a change to aluminium cylinder heads would be beneficial for all competitors, and this decision was then sanctioned by NASCAR.

The Ford aluminium cylinder heads, first cast in 1981 at the Eck Foundry, Wisconsin, and machined at CEP1, included high exhaust ports with each combustion chamber 'roof' posted as cast. Although essentially the inlet porting and combustion chamber was the same as the cast iron Boss 302ci, the cylinder head casting was quite different, as it incorporated the raised port criteria used on the 1972 cast iron 366 NASCAR racing engines. These were very recognisable as derivatives of the basic 1969 and 1970 Boss 302ci Trans-Am component.

The Ford engines used for NASCAR events then employed these Ford-made aluminium cylinder heads, with the casting code E2ZM 6090. They also carried a Ford part number, and were available over the counter at Ford dealers throughout the USA.

AUSTRALIAN NASCAR BLOCKS

The original 366 NASCAR racing blocks, made between 1969 and 1972 for testing purposes, Pro-Stock, and NASCAR racing, were made using prototype tooling. The later versions, especially, had been proven very reliable, and nearing the end of 1972, the Car Research Office, Product Development Group, considered it prudent to manufacture more, using proper tooling. The following letter, dated December 18, 1972, was sent to upper management:

To: Mr DB Eames, Mr TL Tlusty
Cc: Mr J Balcerowiak, Mr RM Corn, Mr LH Morse, Mr TY Wu

Subject: Siamesed, Square Bore 351-C Cylinder Block for OHO Parts Application.

Due to the overwhelming success of the 366 CID engine in drag racing events, we recommend immediate release of a 351-C type cylinder block with (4) bolt mains, and a siamesed, square bore configuration.

This is the type of block that Barry Poole campaigned at the Supernationals. We have disassembled this engine, and although it has had only a limited amount of usage, there are no indications of any future problems with this component. Also, Mr Bud Moore has campaigned a block of this type at various tracks for 1600 miles of NASCAR racing, with no adverse problems.

We have gathered preliminary information relative to casting and machining costs. These figures are based on an estimated FPV of 1000 units minimum, as an economical volume:

Casting tooling: New water jacket core boxes: $80,000
Casting cost: Estimate includes burden for core scrap.
Casting scrap and special handling: $80-$100 each.
Machining cost: At full burden rate: $12.85 each.

You will note that if the $80,000 tooling cost were amortised over 1000 blocks (for example), the final manufacturing cost would be in the area of $173 minimum per block. This would make the task difficult to contain in a competitive price in the market place. We strongly recommend that you initiate a formal request to obtain a manufacturing cost study analysis, to determine the exact implications of marketing a block of this nature, and survey the possibility of Engine Division absorbing part of the tooling, for possible application of this cylinder block.

We can accept a program for 1973 to investigate the feasibility of this concept.

Charles E Gray, Jr

This request was considered, but ultimately rejected, leaving just the remaining stock of XH prefix coded NASCAR blocks available for the foreseeable future. Between late 1969 and mid-1972, 250 blocks of this type were made with semi-finished bores, so as to be capable of accommodating a 4in or 4.080in bore, although only approximately 200 passed inspection and were deemed usable. With the certain knowledge, at the end of 1972, that NASCAR intended to reduce the capacity to 358ci for 1973, Bud Moore had either to reduce the strokes of the existing engines, or obtain new blocks, and use a 4.030in bore. However, in the event, in the mid-1970s, when he was assisting Ford Vice President Don Tope and his son, Warren, with the maintenance of the Boss 302ci Trans-Am Mustang, he mentioned that stocks of 366 Cleveland NASCAR blocks were depleting rapidly, and both he and other car team owners only had very limited numbers remaining. He asked of the likelihood of him procuring new blocks to ease the situation.

As a result of this enquiry, with full approval from upper management at Ford USA, Don Tope subsequently took the decision to enter into a private venture, and have a quantity of blocks made in Australia where production of the Cleveland block was imminent. Ford Australia agreed to help, and requested that all the original NASCAR block and coring pattern work be sent out to Australia for inspection, enabling it to determine its compatibility with its block casting process. On arrival, it was noted that not only was the coring in a poor state, it was designed to suit the 'oil sand' process, and not the CO_2 process, as used by Ford Australia. The difference between the two processes being that the CO_2 method froze the sand, whereas the oil sand method required it to be cured with heat, in an oven, over approximately 45 minutes. Nevertheless, after re-working the original coring to suit its CO_2 process, as oil sand cores expand when heated,

THE ESSENTIAL SOURCE BOOK

while CO2 'chemically frozen' cores do not, Ford Australia was able to make the special blocks.

Two hundred 366 NASCAR blocks, marked XE-192540, were made in two runs of 100 for Don Tope, with the first being cast in December 1975, and machined in early 1976, while the second run was undertaken later in the same year. The machining line at Geelong was incapable of machining four-bolt main caps. Therefore, after the inner two had been processed, the blocks were removed from the line, and placed on a radial drill, and the outer two main cap bolt holes were drilled and tapped in the block, using the holes already drilled in the main caps as a guide. The blocks were then returned to the line, and the main bearing tunnel bores machined, at which point the caps were specific to that particular block, in the numbered order as per normal practice. The increased toughness of the Ford high nickel cast iron made it necessary to decrease the cutting speed, in order to avoid reducing the tool service life. The special nodular iron main caps for these blocks were made in the USA, and shipped to Australia. Two shipments of 366 blocks were sent to the USA, in 1976, where they became available to any interested buyers, and proved to be highly successful. The blocks were fully machined in Australia, although the bores were only finished to a 3.990in diameter, as most race teams preferred to finish the bores themselves.

By 1980, the Don Tope consignment had been sold, and when Michael Kranefuss, as head of Ford's racing operations, began attending NASCAR events, he was frequently approached by Ford racers requesting 366 NASCAR blocks. As a result of these enquiries, and as Ford Australia was still producing Cleveland engines, Ford USA SVO engineer, Rodney Girolami, began negotiations, regarding them producing some more NASCAR blocks for the American market. An agreement was reached, and Ford Australia made all new coring patterns. In March, 1982, 500 NASCAR blocks, marked XE-192540, were cast in batches of between 50 and 70 from Ford's AC grade cast iron, with an additional 5 per cent nickel content. As the usual 3 per cent machining scrap rate had to be taken into account, an approximate total of 525 blocks were made for this order. The fully machined main caps continued to be imported from the USA. The fully machined blocks, with semi-finished undersize bores, were shipped to the USA, where they became available to racers in June 1982. They were bored to the usual 4.000 or 4.030in, to obtain the 358ci, and used in NASCAR racing by Ernie Elliot Inc, Woods Brothers Racing, Bud Moore Engineering, and Junnie Dunlavy.

However, it soon became apparent there was something drastically wrong with these blocks, as the bore walls began failing in much the same way as they had done early in 1972. When Ford USA was informed of the problem, its engineers 'Sonorayed' or ultrasonically tested all the remaining blocks, to check the bore wall thickness. They found there was major core shift of up to $1/8$in in many of the blocks, which, in a worst-case scenario, meant the finished bore wall thickness, in some areas, could be down to little more than $1/8$in, which was inadequate for this most arduous application. As a result, they were all categorised from best to worst, and serialised in a book, so that whenever a block was ordered by a race team, they were always sent the best of the remainder. Had the batch of 500 NASCAR blocks from Ford Australia been successful, orders for more similar blocks would have doubtless followed, as overall, they were extremely good, and completed at a very reasonable cost. The Don Tope blocks had not cracked in the bores with hard racing use, while the later batch of 500, made in 1982, with the all-new coring was unsuccessful, due to the core shift problem. This was the sole reason SVO rejected them, and the remaining 300 were shipped back to Australia as soon as possible, to allow Ford USA to claim a credit. As a result of this episode, SVO went on to develop what became known as the 'Clevor' E3ZM-6010, a marked block which was based on the 351ciW, but with the advantages of the smaller diameter main bearings and lower deck height of the Cleveland block.

In later years, when some Australian-made 302ci and 351ci engines were stripped down for repair or rebuild, they were found to have XE-192540 blocks. These items are very rare, as they are amongst the 300 NASCAR blocks returned to Ford Australia. Then Ford Australia, as a means of utilising the stock, subsequently either sold them as service replacement block or assembled them into engines using its 'build ahead stocks' of parts, in 1982, and fitted them into Falcons, Fairlanes, and LTDs. Despite the fact that these blocks were considered to have major core shift problems, and were unsuitable for racing purposes, there was nothing to suggest they would not be perfectly satisfactory in road-going applications. While the block and main caps were drilled and tapped to accept four bolts for racing applications, after being returned to Australia, only the two large diameter bolts were fitted, as this was perfectly adequate for road cars. Also, to put the extra outer two main cap bolts in would have involved a new release specification, along with a procedure change on the assembly line.

FORD CATALOGUE

The following booklet, *How to Build a 351ci Ford Pro-Stock Pinto*, first distributed in the early 1970s, is reproduced by kind permission of The Ford Motor Company. My very grateful thanks go to retired Engine Engineering engineer Mr Lee Morse for supplying a pristine copy for this publication.

CLEVELAND V8 RACING HISTORY IN NASCAR & PRO-STOCK

FORD PRO-STOCK PINTO

HOW TO BUILD A 351C

CHASSIS AND ENGINE RECOMMENDATIONS THAT CAN BE APPLIED TO OTHER ALL-OUT COMPETITION MACHINES

THE ESSENTIAL SOURCE BOOK

To obtain information regarding rules, classes, race dates, etc., contact the respective sanctioning bodies listed below:

I. Governing body for all automobile competition in the United States:
    ACCUS/FIA Automobile Competition Committee for the U.S., FIA
        330 Vanderbilt Motor Parkway
        Hauppauge, L.I., N.Y. 11787
        AC 516/582-4040

II. Drag Racing:
    NHRA . . . . . National Hot Rod Association
        10639 Riverside Drive
        North Hollywood, California 91602
        AC 213/877-2751
    AHRA . . . . . American Hot Rod Association
        11030 Granada Lane
        Overland Park, Kansas 66211
        AC 913/649-9010
    IHRA . . . . International Hot Rod Association
        P.O. Box 3029
        Bristol, Tennessee 37620
        AC 615/764-1161

III. Stock Car Racing:
    NASCAR . . National Association of Stock Car Auto Racing
        P.O. Bin K
        Daytona Beach, Florida 32015
        AC 904/253-0611

    USAC . . . United States Auto Club
        4910 West 16th Street
        Speedway, Indiana 46224
        AC 317/244-7637

    ARCA . . Automobile Racing Club of America
        3201 Glenwood Avenue
        Toledo, Ohio 43610
        AC 419/244-7632

IV. Sports Car Racing:
    SCCA . . Sports Car Club of America, Inc.
        P.O. Box 22476
        Denver, Colorado 80222
        AC 303/758-6080

    IMSA . . International Motor Sports Association
        P.O. Box 805
        Fairfield, Connecticut 06430
        AC 203/259-5233

V. Off-Road Racing:
    NORRA . . National Off-Road Racing Association
        1616 Victory Blvd., Suite 200
        Glendale, California 91201
        AC 213/245-1033

CLEVELAND V8 RACING HISTORY IN NASCAR & PRO-STOCK

PRO STOCK DRAG RACING

WHERE IT'S AT

Introduction	1
Building An All Competition Engine	2
351C-4V-CJ-H.O.-BOSS Comparison	3-5
Basic Engine Building Techniques	6-7
Major Component Modifications	7-23
Building A Pro-Stock Chassis	24-34
Body Sheetmetal	24-26
Front Suspension	26-28
Driveline	28-30
Rear Axle	30-33
Rear Suspension	33-34
Wheels and Tires	34
Blueprint Specifications	35-36
Aftermarket Parts	Inside Rear Cover

Drag racing attracts more spectators . . . and more participants . . . than any other form of motorsports. The "Pro Stock" class is one of the three most popular forms of drag racing (the others being Dragster and Funny Car classes) . . . which are also categorized as "professional" classes. They're professional because of the highly modified race machines involved, the large purses that go to the winners and the expert driving ability required to race successfully at this level of competition

The Pro Stock class has great appeal to spectators, because it closely resembles a "stock" car as the name implies. Stock appearing seats, dash and interior trim must be in place. The body, although re-worked, must basically be in the stock configuration. Engine, transmission, driveline and suspension components can be highly modified to achieve maximum performance and durability. <u>For precise rules of sanctioning bodies, check their latest rule book.</u>

The Pinto has proven very popular . . . and very competitive in Pro Stock drag racing. "Dyno" Don Nicholson, Bob Glidden, Gapp and Roush, Barrie Poole, Ken Dondero and Dick Brannan are just a few of many heavy Ford runners. Their powerplant is a BOSS 351 CID Cleveland engine. And you'll find in reading this book that the vast majority of performance modifications involve <u>stock Ford parts or Ford "Off Highway Operation" (OHO) parts.</u>

These parts have been designed and tested by Ford engineers. The parts have also been used in competition to prove they work. The result is maximum performance; and minimum use of exotic expensive pieces.

PLEASE NOTE:

This book is expressly written to assist in the building of a Pro Stock Pinto. Much of this information can obviously be applied to other "drag" <u>race</u> classes such as Modified Production and Gas . . . or some "oval track" or "road racing" classes. These are "Off Highway Operation" (OHO) all-out competition vehicles designed to be used on sanctioned race courses. No other applications are intended or implied.

To emphasize this point, we'd like to remind you that . . Federal law restricts the removal or modification of any part of federally required emission control systems on a car or truck.*

In addition, certain states make it a misdemeanor to disconnect, modify or alter any required emission control system. Racing vehicles that are NOT used on public highways may be exempt from such prohibitions. Check the law of your home state.

*

Section 1857f-1 of Title II of the Clean Air Act, as amended 42 USC s1857f-1 et seq provides that the following acts and the causing thereof are prohibited

". . . for any person to remove or render inoperative any device or element of design installed on or in a motor vehicle or motor vehicle engine in compliance with regulations under this title prior to its sale and delivery to the ultimate purchaser, or for any manufacturer or dealer knowingly to remove or render inoperative any such device or element of design after such sale and delivery to the ultimate purchaser."

The Clean Air Act defines "motor vehicle" as a self-propelled vehicle designed for transporting persons or property on a street or highway.

OFF HIGHWAY OPERATION PARTS

Ford Motor Company markets a limited number of O.H.O. performance parts. They are clearly labeled "Off Highway Operation" and include one or both of the following notices:

O.H.O. Parts Warranty Notice

These parts are intended for competition use only, and as such carry no warranty either expressed or implied, of merchantability or fitness or otherwise. Installation of these parts in a vehicle will void the vehicle warranty.

O.H.O. Parts Emission Notice

This part has been designed for off highway applications only, since installation may impair your vehicle's emission control performance. This part should not be installed in any vehicle to be used on a street or highway.

© Copyright Car Corporation

THE ESSENTIAL SOURCE BOOK

BUILDING AN ALL-OUT COMPETITION 351C BOSS ENGINE

1971 Boss 351 Cleveland Engine

Features...

- 4-bolt main bearing caps
- High strength forged con rods (with 180,000 psi bolt)
- Large "canted" valves (2.19" intake / 1.71" exhaust)
- Single-groove hardened keepers
- Hardened and ground push rods
- Tapered I.D. piston pins
- Adjustable valve train with 7/16" stud
- "Quench" polyangle combustion chamber
- Forged aluminum 11.1:1 pop-up pistons
- Aluminum over/under intake manifold
- High lift, solid lifter camshaft

With this kind of pedigree, it is obvious that the 1971 BOSS 351C engine has great potential for all-out competition. For instance, it can be modified to run very competitively in many race classes such as:

Drag Racing	Oval Track	Road Racing
• Pro-Stock	• Modified	• Sedan
• Modified Prod.	• Late Model Stock	• Sports Car
• Gas		

Although this book specifically covers Pro-Stock Drag Racing, most of the information can be applied to other classes by changing such things as induction and camshaft. Before starting any modifications, it is most important to check with sanctioning bodies to see what is legal for various classes. See inside front cover for addresses of most prominent groups.

2

CLEVELAND V8 RACING HISTORY IN NASCAR & PRO-STOCK

IMPORTANT 351 CLEVELAND ENGINE COMPARISONS 4V...CJ...BOSS...HO

This section compares 351C-4V, CJ, BOSS and HO engines to help you know what's involved in building an all-out competition engine from a completely stock engine, short block or components. The 351-2V is not included because it requires extreme modifications.

The best engine assembly to modify for all-out competition is the 1971 BOSS 351C. Complete engine assemblies can no longer be purchased from Ford Dealers however, because only current production engines can be bought as complete assemblies through the Ford Parts Division. Therefore, unless you have a good used engine, the choice boils down to individual components or a 1971 short block assembly (block, crank, rods, pistons, cam and timing chain). Since the cam and pistons must be replaced, individual parts may be the best way to go.

Then again, you may be able to pick up a good used 351-4V, CJ, or HO. They require a little more modification than a '71 BOSS 351, but are a definite possibility. The "Comparison Chart" points out differences. To assist in reading the chart, here is a short background on the 351C.

351C Development

The 351C came on the scene with 1970 models, topped with 2V or 4V induction. Two barrel heads had "open" combustion chambers, whereas 4V heads used "quench" chambers.

Combustion Chambers

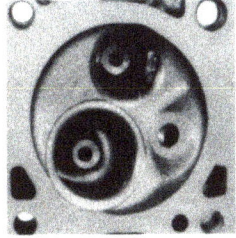
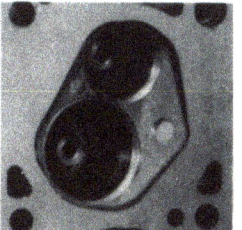

Open: '71 CJ, '72 4V and HO, '73 4V

Quench: '71 4V and BOSS

Quench chambers encourage a swirling action of the incoming air-fuel charge. This improves mixture... especially at low rpm... when the mixture travels at a relatively low velocity. This causes a more complete burning of the fuel and better low rpm torque.

Unfortunately, quench chambers tend to affect emissions adversely; especially hydrocarbons. That's because the quench area remains relatively cool. So cold in fact, that when the spark plug ignites the mixture, causing a flame front to move across the chamber towards the quench area, the flame may be exinguished near the end of its travel. The result is unburned fuel.

Open chamber designs, on the other hand, exhibit better emission characteristics. There is no quench area and valves are less shrouded; thereby encouraging excellent breathing. However, you sacrifice some of the good low rpm torque advantage associated with the quench chamber. This, of course, isn't too important with most off highway engines.

As of this date, Ford has not developed a special pop-up piston that will give 12- or 13.0:1 ratio with open chamber heads. Thus, the quench head is recommended. However, this doesn't preclude use of open chamber heads. If you elect to go this route, it simply means you will have to work with a piston manufacturer to develop an appropriate piston design.

Four barrel heads also had larger valves and ports, and a bit hotter hydraulic cam to handle the extra breathing. Both of these engines were available in 1971... basically unchanged. The BOSS 351 was made available with 1971 models and in mid-year (May 1971) the 351C-Cobra Jet appeared.

Production Pistons

Pop-Up
(1971 BOSS) Forged

Flat Top
(71-72-73 CJ) - Cast
(1972 H.O.) - Forged

Heads

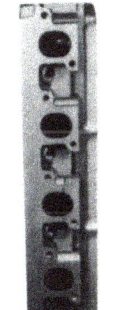

| 2V | 4V-Boss CJ | 2V | 4V-Boss CJ |

EXHAUST   INTAKE

3

THE ESSENTIAL SOURCE BOOK

1971 4V and CJ Comparison

The stock CJ hydraulic cam had more duration and overlap than the 4V stick. CJ blocks also feature 4-bolt main caps. CJ heads used the "open" 2V combustion chamber design, but retained the larger valves and ports of the 4V head. 4V engines used a model 4300-A Motorcraft carburetor, with a standard Holley-Motorcraft manifold bolt pattern. CJ engines, on the other hand, used a model 4300-D Motorcraft carburetor. The "D" model carburetor features small primaries and large secondaries . . . giving rise to a "spread bore" manifold bolt pattern.

Carburetor Bolt Patterns

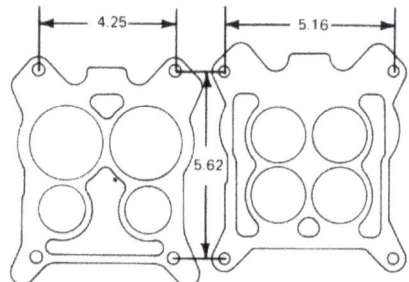

Spread Bore (Model 4300-D)   Standard (Model 4300 A)

1972 4V and CJ Comparison

This one is tricky. The Cobra Jet name was dropped in '72, as was the '71 4V design. The Cobra Jet engine design was retained in '72, but is called a 351C-4V. In other words, a 1972 351C-4V is the same as a 1971 351C Cobra Jet. Except for one small change. There is a 4-degree cam retard in valve timing specs for '72.

1971 Boss and 1972 H.O. Comparison

Again we have a name change. The '71 351 BOSS engine was called a 351C-H.O. in 1972. There are also major differences in piston and cylinder head design. 1971 BOSS heads use "quench" combustion chambers. However, the 1972 H.O. heads are the "open" type . . . but retain 1971 sized ports and valves. Both heads are machined to accept mechanical valve train components. (4V and CJ are machined for hydraulic cams only.) 1972 H.O. engines use a forged flat-top piston (8.8:1 nominal compression ratio), whereas 1971 BOSS engines used a forged pop-up piston (11.3:1 nominal compression ratio). The stock 1971 cam provides increased duration and overlap, compared to the 1972 grind.

Rocker Arm Pedestals

351C Pedestal   BOSS 302 and
                             BOSS 351C Pedestal

1972-1973 4V and CJ Comparison

Except for a slightly larger combustion chamber, which lowered the "nominal" compression ratio to 7.9:1, these engines are almost identical. But the names changed once more. All 1973 351C-4V engines are called 351 "CJ" again!

1971-1972 Component Comparison 351C . . . 4V-CJ-Boss-H.O.
(Nominal inches except as shown)

	1971		1972	
	4V and CJ	BOSS	4V/CJ	H.O.
Rear Oil Seal	Rope type	Split lip	Same as '71 CJ	Same as '71 Boss
Valve Spring	285 lbs. @ 1.32 open	315 lb. @ 1.32 open	Same as '71 CJ	Same as '71 Boss
Valve Sp. Retainer	Compatible with multi-Groove keeper	Compatible with single groove keeper	Same as '71 CJ	Same as '71 Boss
Valve Spring Key	Multi-groove	Single groove-hardened	Same as '71 CJ	Same as '71 Boss
Valve Stem Seal	Production 351C	Production 429 with shorter skirt for improved lubrication	Same as '71 CJ	Same as '71 Boss
Valve Spring Seat	None required	Stamped Steel	None required	Same as '71 Boss
Push Rod	Production	Hardened and ground	Same as '71 CJ	Same as '71 Boss
Push Rod Guide Plt.	None Required	Sames as 302 Boss	None required	Same as '71 Boss

CLEVELAND V8 RACING HISTORY IN NASCAR & PRO-STOCK

1971-1972 Component Comparison 351C . . . 4V-CJ-BOSS H.O.
(Continued)

	1971		1972	
	4V and CJ	**BOSS**	**4V/CJ**	**H.O.**
Camshaft	Hydraulic 4V-duration 266° I/270° E overlap 34° lift 0.427" CJ-duration 270° I/290° E overlap 46° lift 0.480"/0.488"	Mechanical duration 290° I and E overlap 58° lift 0.477"	Same as '71 CJ, except valve events retarded 4°	Mechanical duration 275° I & E overlap 35° lift 0.491"
Tappets	Hydraulic	Mechanical-internal metering	Same as '71 CJ	Same as '71 Boss
Crankshaft	Cast iron	Cast iron-selected for hardness (90% nodularity)	Same as '71 CJ	Same as '71 Boss
Damper	0.10 inertia -cast iron hub -cast iron inertia ring -non-bonded elastic member -28.2 oz-in unbalance	0.14 inertia -nodular iron hub -wider cast iron inertia ring -bonded elastic member -27.3 oz.-in.unbalance	Same as '71 CJ	Same as '71 Boss
Flywheel	Cast Iron 28.2 oz.-in. unbalance	Nodular Iron-27.3 oz.-in. unbalance	Same as '71 CJ	Same as '71 Boss
Cylinder Block	4V-2 bolt main caps CJ-4 bolt main caps	4 bolt main caps selected for hardness	Same as '71 CJ	Same as '71 Boss
Cylinder Head	4V-Quench chamber 64.6—67.6 cc -non adjustable rocker arm pedestal CJ-Open chamber 73.9-76.9 cc -induction hardened exhaust valve seats Otherwise same as 4V	Quench chamber 64.6-67.6 cc Otherwise same as '71 4V, except rocker arm pedestal machined for mechanical camshaft	Same as '71 CJ	Open chamber 73.9-76.9 cc Otherwise same as '71 Boss
Cyl. Head Gasket	4V Production composition CJ Reintz Repa comp. for 100 ft-lb torque	Reintz special comp. for 120 ft.-lb. torque	Same as '71 CJ	Similar to '71 Boss
Intake Valve	2.19" dia head 11/32" dia solid stem Multi-groove key Sil-Chrome No. 1	2.19 dia head 11/32" dia solid stem Single groove key Sil-Chrome No. 1	Same as '71 CJ	Same as '71 Boss
Exhaust Valve	1.71" dia head 11/32" dia solid stem Multi-groove key 21-4N Steel	1.71" dia head 11/32" dia solid stem Single groove key 21-4N Steel	Same as '71 CJ	Same as '71 Boss
Rocker Arm Stud	5/16 bolt	7/16" threaded stud	Same as '71 CJ	Same as '71 Boss
Rocker Arm Fulcrum	"T" shaped-non adj.	Cylindrical-adjustable	Same as '71 CJ	Same as '71 Boss
Rocker Arm	CJ stamped-high strength 4V Production	Stamped high strength	Same as '71 CJ	Same as '71 Boss
Connecting Rod	1041-H Forged Steel 3/8" nut and bolt	1041-H Forged Steel -shot peened -magnafluxed -improved durability 180,000 psi 3/8" nut and bolt	Same as '71 CJ	Same as '71 Boss
Piston	Cast Aluminum-flat top CJ-9.0:1 CR 4V-10.7:1 CR	Forged Aluminum-pop up 11.1:1 CR	Same as '71 CJ except CR is 9.0:1	Forged Aluminum-flat top 9.2:1 CR
Piston Pin	0.912" dia. I.D. non-tapered	0.912" dia I.D. tapered	Same as '71 CJ	Same as '71 Boss
Con Rod Bearings	Over-plated copper/lead w/increased eccentricity	Same as CJ	Same as '71 CJ	Same as '71 Boss
Oil Pan Assembly	Production w/welded windage baffle	Same as CJ	Same as '71 CJ	Same as '71 Boss
Oil Lever Indicator	Calibrated for 5 qts.	Calibrated for 6 qts.	Same as '71 CJ	Same as '71 Boss
Intake Manifold	Cast Iron-over/under	Cast Aluminum-over/under	Same as '71 CJ	Same as '71 Boss
Carburetor	4V-Autolite Model 4300-A CJ-Autolite Model 4300-D w/spread bore pattern	4V Autolite Model 4300-D	Same as '71 CJ	Same as '71 Boss except with different calibration.
Distributor	4V-Single point dual diaphragm CJ-Dual point dual diaphragm	Same as CJ, except for calibration	Same as '71 4V	Same as '71 Boss
Rocker Arm Covers	Stamped Steel	Cast Aluminum	Same as '71 CJ	Same as '71 Boss
Air Cleaner	Ram air-optional	Ram air	Ram air not avail.	Ram air not available
Oil Fill	5 qt. SAE 10W-30	6 qts. SAE 40 (summer) 6 qts. SAE 20 (winter)	Same as '71 CJ	Same as '71 Boss

THE ESSENTIAL SOURCE BOOK

BASIC ENGINE BUILDING TECHNIQUES

Although this book is written for the serious racer, who generally knows all about engine building, these "basics" are included for the newcomers to make sure they get off on the right foot. Which to put it simply is . . . "pull the engine and blueprint."

> NOTE: Standard procedures for pulling an engine from a chassis, or standard servicing operations are not covered. The only procedures explained pertain to special performance modifications. Specifications and part numbers are included in the back of the book.
>
> If you need service procedures, contact:
>
> Ford Product Information Center
> 12263 Market Street
> Livonia, Michigan 48150
> Telephone (313) 261-6990
>
> If you need Ford Service Manuals, contact:
> Helm, Inc.
> P. O. Box 07150
> Detroit, Michigan 48207
> Telephone (313) 871-6606

Mating Surfaces

With your 351C engine out of the chassis, and disassembled down to the short block, check all mating surfaces between heads and block . . . and between intake manifold and heads to check for any signs of warpage or leaking. Look for patterns on the gaskets or metal surfaces which might indicate that a complete seal was not made . . . or that air, compression, or water leaks might have been present.

Deck Height

Next, check all deck height readings. You will usually observe minor variations between cylinders. It is desirable to make the heights of each cylinder as close to one another as possible. This can be done by juggling pistons and rods or by milling the block face, if necessary.

The simplest and least expensive way, of course, is to take the rod and piston from a "long" cylinder and swap it for a "shorter" one, making certain that other tolerances such as bore and crankshaft clearances stay within specs. This can be done when the engine is being reassembled.

Clearances

When all deck height readings have been made, take readings on rod side clearance . . . crank end play . . . and rod and main bearing clearances. Side clearance should be checked with a dial indicator or feeler gauge.

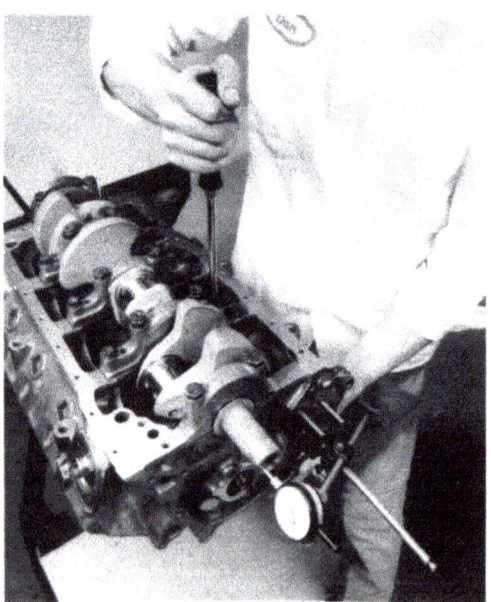

Checking Crankshaft End Play.

Tap the rods lightly to be certain they are fully to one side. Record the readings for each throw, noting those which may be out of the specification range.

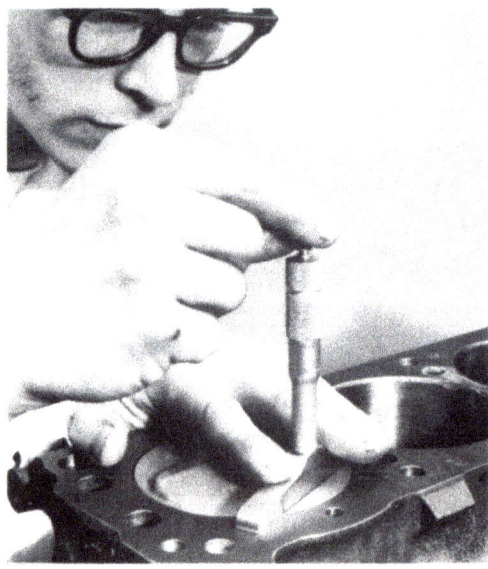

Checking Deck Height

CLEVELAND V8 RACING HISTORY IN NASCAR & PRO-STOCK

If rod side clearance is too low, the inside mating faces of the rods must be cut. To get the clearance desired, take half the amount off each rod.

Be certain you remove metal from the inside facing surfaces of the rods . . . not the fillet side.

This job is usually done with a surface grinder and we recommend you farm it out to a capable machine shop.

To check crankshaft end play, you will again need to use a dial indicating gauge. Position it so that the gauge finger rests lightly on the end of the crank . . . then take a heavy screwdriver and place it between the center main bearing cap or web and the adjacent crankshaft counter weight. Using the screwdriver for leverage, force the crankshaft to the limit of its travel toward the front of the block. Take several readings to be certain you are getting full travel, and record the end play reading. Should crank end play be on the tight side, it will be necessary to remove equal amounts of metal from the two thrust faces of the crankshaft at the center main . . . or . . . remove stock from the front flange surace of the upper and lower thrust bearings. This also should be done by a competent machine shop or speed shop specializing in crankshaft modification.

To check main bearing and rod bearing crankshaft journal clearances, use a micrometer. If air-type gauging equipment is available, by all means use it.

Should you find your stock clearances on the tight side, you will have to have the crankshaft bearing surfaces polished to remove the desired amount of metal. Journal roundness and taper must be within .0003-inches. "Hour glassing" must be avoided.

Be sure you carefully mark the number of thousandths to come off of each throw or main to bring it up to your specifications.

Rods and Pistons

With these clearances checked and noted, you are now ready to complete the engine teardown job. Be certain that you mark each piston, rod and bearing with the cylinder number or bearing number so that you know the position of each part removed. Before pushing the pistons and rods out of the bores, be sure to cover the exposed threads on the rod bolts with rubber spark plug insulator caps or pieces of rubber tubing. If you should scratch a cylinder wall you'll have an oil and compression leak and a potential source of failure. It is also easy to scratch a crankshaft throw if you aren't careful and don't cover the rod bolt threads.

With the pistons removed from the bores, check the bores for roundness, taper or "barrel" and check piston-to-wall clearances. The best approach to this is to use a dial bore gauge, or an inside and outside micrometer. Record the readings for each cylinder.

If you find your clearances are tight, hone the cylinders to get the desired clearance. Honing should be done with a No. 725 Sunnen stone to obtain a 12-16 micro-finish and a 45 degree cross-pattern. Cylinders are to be free of tool marks and should be completely honed throughout their length. Honing ridges and other surface imperfections are not acceptable. Maximum out-of-round should be .001-inch, maximum taper .001-inch, and maximum barrel or hourglass .0005 in. When you have measured and recorded your piston-to-wall clearances, the last block check should be the crankshaft bore. You want to be certain that all crankshaft bores and bearings are in as close to perfect alignment as you can amke them and the only way to check it is by having a professional speed shop run a line bore check for you. They have the equipment to check and correct any possible misalignment.

Miscellaneous Machining

At this point, you are usually finished with your teardown and tolerance checks. Now is the time for any machine work that may be needed such as milling the faces to correct a deck height problem.

MAJOR COMPONENT MODIFICATIONS

Block

Two blocks are recommended, both featuring 4-bolt main caps. The first is D1ZZ-6010-D, which was used for '71 BOSS and '72 H.O. engines. The second is D1ZZ-6010-A, which is used on '71-'72-'73 "CJ" engines. The "CJ" block uses a "rope" seal at the rear main and thus has a small pin in the rear main cap to keep the seal in place. For race applications, this pin must be removed and a "split lip" seal (D0OZ-6701-A) installed.

The BOSS/HO block currently lists for about $20.00 more, but is designed for a split lip rear seal and thus doesn't have the pin. Otherwise, these two blocks are identical.

Other than cleaning and deburring, the only special work the block requires is a 0.030-inch overbore to 4.030-inch, which when combined with a 3.50 in. stroke gives 357 CID.

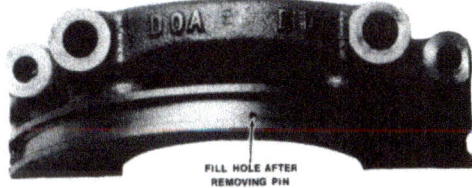

Split Lip Seal - BOSS & H.O. Blocks vs. Rope Seal - "CJ" Block

THE ESSENTIAL SOURCE BOOK

If you're working with a "used" block, the first step is to clean and degrease the block in a hot tank. Remove all threaded and press-fit plugs to assure that all passages are as unrestricted as possible.

NOTE: Some hot tank solutions are very caustic and will attack the metal camshaft bearings. Always check cam bearings after hot tank cleaning.

If you start with a "new" block, hot tanking usually isn't necessary. Once the block is cleaned, rework as follows:

1. Check for cracks and imperfections. Pay particular attention to the oil supply holes of the main bearing caps, the lower skirt of cylinder bores, and around plug holes.

2. Deburr the block in order to remove every sharp edge and smooth down every lumpy spot or bit of casting flash with small hand grinder, files and chamfer tools. This will help assure that small pieces of metal do not break away and close oil passages, or scuff moving surfaces. It also aids in reducing stress areas where cracks are most likely to start. Important areas are cylinder bore chamfer, main bearing bore chamfers, webbing and walls. It is also a good idea to put a small chamfer on stud holes, such as head bolt holes, to prevent the top thread from pulling up when torqued. You don't, of course, touch any finished or machined surface . . . just the sharp edges, and then with great care. A well deburred block is one that you can run your hand around without getting cut or nicked, by any surface, top to bottom.

3. Run a small bottle brush or drill through all oil passages, and a bottoming tap down all bolt holes to clean out foreign deposits.

4. Check alignment and diameter of cylinder bores, main bearing bores and camshaft bores.

5. Overbore block. Do not exceed <u>thirty thousandths</u> as this is a "thin wall" design block.

6. Install crank, rods, pistons and <u>one</u> piston ring to check deck height clearance, and to see that the deck is parallel to centerline of crankshaft. The distance from the crankshaft axis to the block deck surface must be the same, front to rear. If not, machine deck surfaces. <u>Cut the minimum amount necessary to produce a true, flat surface for accurate decking.</u> A final cut is then made to achieve required deck clearance for desired compression ratio.

7. Hone cylinder walls with a 45 degree cross-pattern using No. 725 Sunnen stone (or equivalent) to a 12-16 micro finish and refit pistons with rings.

NOTE: A few years ago, a 25-35 micro-finish was recommended to seat rings quickly, when piston ring manufacturers didn't put a super-fine finish on rings. Today, however, high performance "Moly" rings are barrel-lapped at the factory . . . which is to say that they're put into a bore with lapping compound and worked to a fine finish. Thus, a finer 12-16 micro-finish is recommended with double Moly ring sets (No. 1 and No. 2 rings) or with a Moly top ring and cast iron No. 2 ring.

To further assure excellent bore finish, a "torque plate" should be installed when re-working bores. Installing a plate and tightening it down with head bolts to torque specifications distorts the block (up to .0035") as it will be when the heads are installed. Most high performance machine shops use a torque plate. However, if you're doing the work yourself, you may wish to fabricate one from 1 1/2" thick steel. Cut it to the shape of a head. Machine four cylinder bores (about .060" oversize) and holes for head bolts.

8. Remove pistons and clean complete block with hot, soapy water to remove all foreign particles. Rinse and dry with compressed air.

NOTE: At this point, some engine builders feel that painting the casting surfaces, inside and out, seals the pores and traps any particles that might work loose. If you decide to paint, use a flat primer-type paint that is oil and gas resistant. Apply with small brush to all casting surfaces both inside and out. <u>Do NOT paint any machined or mating surface . . . and use extreme care not to drip paint on bores or into tapped holes.</u>

9. Spray anit-rust lubricant onto all bores, bearing surfaces, deck and timing chain area. Cover block with plastic bag until ready for assembly.

Crankshaft

The recommended crankshaft is the stock 351 BOSS piece, D1ZZ-6303-A. This is a special cast iron crank that has high nodularity, which results in greater strength and fatigue resistance. Of course, as with any race part, it is a good idea to Magnaflux to check for imperfections. Also check straightness, journal diameters, and bearing clearances. Ford, Clevite-77 or Federal-Mogul AP Series premium main bearings (full grooved) are recommended.

Clearances*

Drag	.0035" - .0040"
Road & Oval	.0025" - .0030"

*NOTE: Stack-up of tolerances between stock journal diameter and bearings will give from .0006" - .0040". Select fit bearings or polish journals to achieve recommended clearance. Ford offers "Red" and "Blue" .001" — .002" undersize (thicker) main bearings.

STOCK BALANCER WITH COUNTERWEIGHT — COUNTERWEIGHT REMOVED

Remove Counterweight From Harmonic Balancer When Crankshaft Is Internally Balanced.

CLEVELAND V8 RACING HISTORY IN NASCAR & PRO-STOCK

For regular production usage, the 351 BOSS crank is externally balanced at the flywheel and harmonic damper. However, for race purposes the crank should be internally balanced to reduce weight at each end of the crank and resulting bending moments. If stock 351 BOSS con rods are used, the total bobweight should be 2108.3 grams to achieve internal balance. To compensate for internally balancing the crank, machine the counterweight out of the stock harmonic balancer as illustrated.

Flywheel & Clutch

The recommended flywheel for pro-stock drag racing is a Sema-approved item such as Weber, Hays or Schiefer forged steel piece No. 634-0024. It is designed for 11 inch clutch discs, has 164 teeth and "zero" balance to be compatible with the internally balanced crank. It weighs forty pounds and its inertia momentum acts as a launch pad coming off the line. Road racing and oval track competitors may prefer a lighter flywheel.

NOTE: If you <u>externally</u> balance your crankshaft, use a flywheel such as Schiefer No. 634-0021, which also weighs forty pounds, but has imbalance incorporated. The recommended clutch assembly is one with a .150" thick cover such as Schiefer "Long" Pressure Plate No. 627-0007. It weighs twenty-one pounds, has a 2800 pound pressure plate load and uses 11 inch clutch disc No. 625-0006 that is compatible with a 10-spline, 1 3/8 inch diameter transmission input shaft.

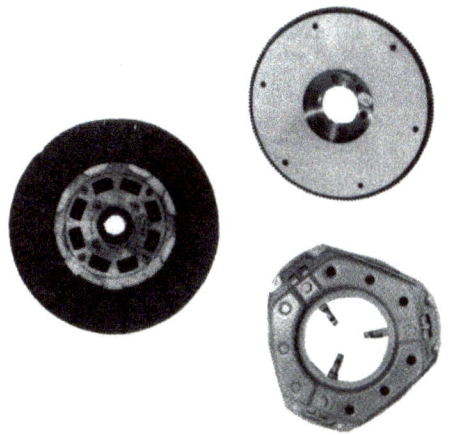

Schiefer Competition Flywheel, Clutch Disc and Pressure Plate.

Connecting Rods

The stock 351 BOSS con rod D1ZZ-6200-A, is the highest strength, highest quality rod ever used in Ford, regular production engines, and can be used in race application to 8,000 rpm. Its premium grade features include being forged from SAE 1041 fine grain steel, and being shot-peened and Magnafluxed at the factory.
Do NOT polish these rods or you will destroy the <u>20,000 psi compressive surface stress created by shot-peening, unless you have them reshot-peened at a high-performance shop after polishing.</u>

These rods use premium grade bolts (D1ZZ-6214-A) and nuts (D1ZZ-6212-A). The bolts feature 3/8 in. diameter threads that are rolled after heat treat and a head-to-shank radius that is worked after heat treat, plus a 180,000 psi tensile strength to withstand high torque specifications. The nuts feature specially designed threads to allow very precise torque settings that won't loosen at high rpm.

Before installing the rods, check the big end for roundness on professional equipment such as a Sunnen-type rod machine. In order to get an accurate reading, torque the bolts to 50-55 ft.-lb. (with oil under nut) so the rods will be stressed as installed in engine. Con rod bore I.D. must measure 2.4361"— 2.4365" to correct bore distortion and achieve adequate bearing crush. Use Ford, Clevite-77 or Federal-Mogul <u>premium</u> aluminum bearings. Ford offers "Red" and "Blue" .001" - .002" undersize (thicker) con rod bearings.

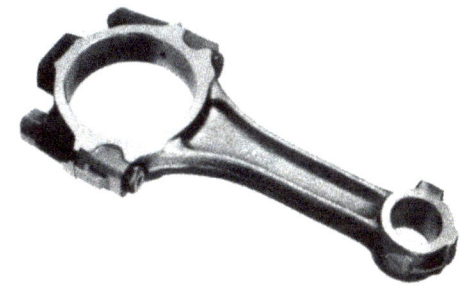

351 BOSS Premium Con Rod

Alternate Con Rods

For applications other than Pro-Stock drag racing, or for higher rpm capability, you may wish to consider one of the special after-market manufacturer's con rods. For instance, "MR. ROD" makes an excellent steel rod. However, the crank journal will have to be ground down from 2.311" to 2.100". If you prefer a lighter aluminum rod, there are a number of excellent pieces to choose from (Brooks, Forged True, Howard, etc.).

Clearances

Steel — Drag	.0030" - .0035"
Steel — Road & Oval	.0025" - .0030"
Aluminum — Drag only	.0040" - .0045"

NOTE: Stack-up of tolerances between stock journal diameter and bearings will give from .0008" - .0040". Select fit bearings or polish journals to achieve recommended clearances.

THE ESSENTIAL SOURCE BOOK

PISTONS - RINGS - PINS

Pistons

The recommended pistons are TRW No. L-2348-F . . . 0.030'' oversize (4.030''). When checking diameter, measure across the skirted sides, at a point level with the centerline of the piston pin. These are forged aluminum pop-up pistons that give a nominal compression ratio of 12.0:1 . . . with a deck clearance of 0.010'', a combustion chamber volume of 66.1 cc and head gasket volume of 8.00 cc (with head gasket D3ZZ-6051-A). In order to maintain a minimum piston-to-valve clearance of 0.100'', that is about the maximum CR possible, without flycutting pistons. For Pro Stock racing, a 12.5:1 CR is recommended, which can be achieved by slabbing the heads to obtain a 63.1 cc chamber volume and then flycutting the pistons .030'' to maintain .100'' valve clearance. Do not reduce piston dome thickness below .150''.

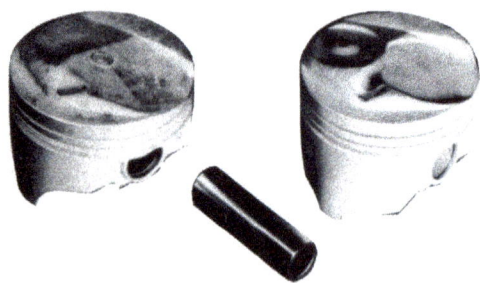

Stock TRW Piston on Left; Flycut TRW Piston on Right.

Alternate Piston

Those engine builders who like a long con rod to reduce angularity with the piston at BDC should consider Ford's .020'' oversize "Competition ONLY" piston D1ZX-6108-B. Although originally developed for the 302 "Trans Am" mills, it has similarities to the 351C TRW piston, such as identical tops and being made from forged aluminum. However, it has some differences that require special attention.

	302 COMPETITION ONLY PISTON D1ZX-6108-B	TRW PISTON No. L-2348-F
Con Rod Length	6.065''	5.780''
Weight	530 grams	510 grams
Compression Height	1.360''	1.645''
Diameter	4.020''	4.030''
CID	354.75	357

Longer con rolds are available from a number of excellent manufacturers such as MR. ROD.

Piston to Valve Clearance

The procedure for checking is usually done by placing flattened modeling clay atop the piston area where the valves operate. Install the head gasket, head, valve train, etc., set tappet clearance at zero and torque all bolts to specifications. Turn the engine over manually two revolutions and then remove the heads. The modeling clay will be compressed, showing the indentations caused by the valves. Carefully slice through each indented section, at the point of greatest compression, with a sharp knife or blade. With a machinist's scale, measure the thickness of the clay. This will tell you your clearance between valve and piston.

An alternate method of checking piston-to-valve clearance is by using a dial indicator on top of the valve spring retainer. The usual procedure is to place the valve in position in the head, using an extremely light, flexible spring to hold it in place. Install the head gasket, head, valve train, etc., set tappet clearance at zero and torque all bolts to specifications. With the cylinder on the overlap cycle, start the piston moving upward. At about 40 degrees before TDC, start checking the valve clearance by depressing the valve manually until the valve bottoms on the piston. Check your gauge reading and record clearance. Do this every five degrees until you have reached 40 degrees ATDC. This procedure will tell you the minimum clearance point in the overlap cycle . . . and you will then be able to tell how much to relieve your pistons.

It is recommended that you check No. 1 and No. 6 cylinder to be sure that minimum clearance is met. It only takes one bent or broken valve to put you out of action, so be certain you have at least .070'' clearance with "zero" lash.

NOTE: TRW No. L-2348-F pop-up pistons for the 351C engine sold after November 1, 1972 feature a fire slot in the dome that causes the air-fuel charge to be burned more efficiently, and is worth about 8 Bhp @ 8000 rpm. If you have an earlier set of TRW pistons, add the fire slot with a small grinder.

ROAD RACING AND OVAL engines that operate at extended high rpm should have the piston modified as illustrated to improve lubrication of the piston pin. Drill a small hole in the boss through the oil control groove. Intersect with another small hole drilled up from the piston pin hole. Repeat for opposite side.

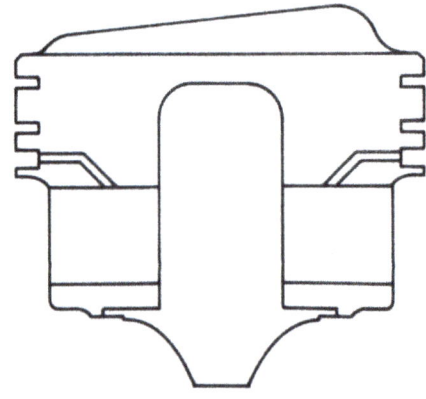

Lubrication Holes Added For Extended High RPM Operation

CLEVELAND V8 RACING HISTORY IN NASCAR & PRO-STOCK

Piston Rings

Choosing piston rings is largely a matter of personal preference. However, remember to order 0.030" oversize. For No. 1 groove, a Moly type is recommended, such as made by "Sealed Power", etc. A cast iron type is recommended for No. 2 groove, such as Ramco, Sealed Power, etc. A Sealed Power No. 3 oil control ring should also be used.

Piston Pins

The stock 351 BOSS piston pin C9ZZ-6135-E is recommended for use with the TRW piston. It features lightweight combined with high strength, and was originally designed for the "LeMans" engines and later used in the Trans Am 302 mills. It is made from SAE 5120 steel, undergoes extensive heat treat, is precision ground and tapered internally at the ends to reduce weight. It weighs 146.5 grams and nominal dimensions are 3.025" x 0.9123". This pin is designed to be <u>pressed</u> into the rod with a .0006 - .0012" interference fit so that it takes a minimum force of 1800 lbs. to move pin. Therefore, although the TRW piston has grooves for "full floating" pin, <u>do NOT modify piston and/or pin for full floating set up</u>. The recommended way to go is the pressed pin route.

Camshaft

Selecting a cam requires <u>precise</u> knowledge of the vehicle it is to be used in and type of competition. Heads, valves, induction, weight, tires, gearing, rpm range, etc., all play a part . . . which means there's no such thing as an all-purpose high performance cam. The trick tip is to consult with one of the many excellent cam manufacturers. Ford offers a super stick that works well in Pro-Stock drag racing. It may have other applications, such as Modified Production drag racing.

A number of specialty high performance cam manufacturers grind Pro Stock sticks. For instance, General Kinetics offers one under part number F5M332-B that works very well.

Ford D1ZX-6250-FA Specifications

Lifter		Intake Events		Exhaust Events		Duration		Lift		Overlap	Identification	
Type	Lash Hot	Open	Close	Open	Close	Intake	Exhaust	Lobe	Valve		Mark	Location
Mech.	.025"	62° BTC	84° ABC	90° BBC	64° ATC	326°	334°	.355"I	.589"	126°	D1ZX -CA	Between last lobe and journal
		18° ATC	35° ABC	45° BBC	13° BTC			.368"E	.612"			

G-K Cam Specifications for F5M332-B

Lifter		Intake Events		Exhaust Events		Duration		Lift		Overlap	Identification	
Type	Lash Hot	Open	Close	Open	Close	Intake	Exhaust	Lobe	Valve		Mark	Location
Mech.	.027"	58° BTC	94° ABC	94° BBC	58° ATC	332°	332°	.370"	.617"	116°	F5M332 -B	Rear of Cam
		16° ATC	52° ABC	52° BBC	16° BTC							

NOTE: (1) Valve lift is computed with 1.73:1 rocker arm ratio (2) The camshaft valve timing figures in "black" reflect actual valve movement, not just theoretical camshaft lobe readings. They are useful in comparing relative performance characteristics of different cams. The figures in the "gray" bar are taken at .100" tappet lift. This is an arbitary reference point on the cam lobe where the rate of movement can easily be read with a dial indicator. This is useful in checking the cam with a degree wheel when it is installed in the engine.

As with any cam installation, it is mandatory to use tappets designed by the cam manufacturer to be compatible with its camshafts. G-K offers kit No. K-20, which includes tappets, valve springs, and retainers.

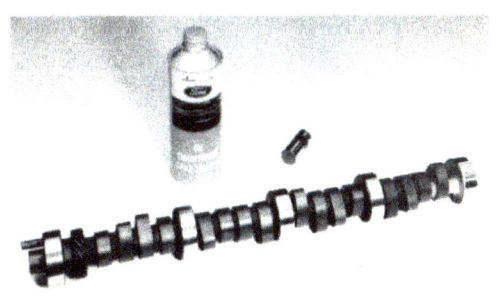

D1ZX-6250-FA Cam Kit

THE ESSENTIAL SOURCE BOOK

The recommended Ford camshaft for Pro-Stock drag racing features 326° / 334° duration and .589" / .612" valve lift. It is only available in cam and tappet kit D1ZX-6250-FA. The kit (cam, tappets and break-in lube) is necessary because of a unique cam lobe and tappet radius design, that makes other cams and tappets non-interchangeable. The tappets have an 80-inch spherical radius, which are compatible with a cam lobe taper of 3-5 minutes. An 80-inch spherical radius reduces contact stress compared to mechanical tappets that have a radius of 50 inches (for use with cam lobe taper of 6-10 minutes).

NOTE: Although these numbers are very small (there are 60 minutes in one degree), the forces involved are extremely large. So, don't try interchanging cam and tappets with other components. It plain flat-out won't work.

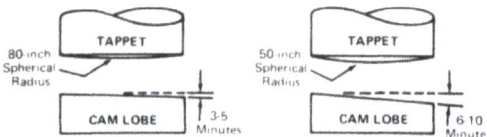

D1ZX-6500-CA TAPPET   OTHER MECHANICAL TAPPETS

This unique tappet is serviced under part number D1ZX-6500-CA. It is not interchangeable with other mechanical tappets, nor can other mechanical tappets be used in place of D1ZX-6500-CA.

NOTE: Do not confuse these mechanical tappets with hydraulic tappets because you can hear its "metering plate" rattle when the tappet is shaken. This metering plate is precision fit to the inside diameter of the tappet bore. The clearance between the O.D. of the metering plate and the I.D. of the tappet bore governs the amount of oil that flows "upstairs" via the pushrod to maintain lubrication of the upper valve train without causing a pressure loss in the oil system.

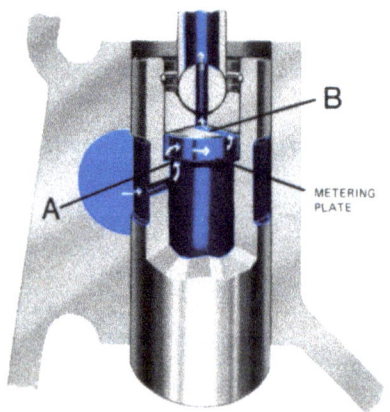

D1ZX-6500-CA "Metering Valve" Mechanical Tappet.

Here is how it works. Oil enters the tappet from the tappet gallery in the block through a hole in an undercut area of the tappet. It travels, unmetered, up the body of the lifter, passing through slot "A" on the underside of the metering plate. Oil is then precision metered around the O.D. of the metering plate, through slot "B" on the top face of the metering plate, and then to the pushrod seat . . . then up the pushrod to the rocker arms.

Cam Installation

When installing a new cam, there are several precautions that you must take. The first few minutes of run-in for a new cam are the most critical moments of its life. Proper initial lubrication is absolutely vital. You must use a can of Ford Oil Conditioner (Part No. D2AZ-19579-A) to completely cover all cam bearings, lobe surfaces, and tappet faces, prior to installation. Page 11 shows a cam and tappet with the Ford Oil Conditioner.

If Ford's three-piece valve spring DOZX-6A511-A and D1FZ-6250-FA camshaft are used, install the springs at a height of 1.80" and run-in at 2000-2500 rpm for 15-20 minutes. After break-in, re-adjust spring height to specified 1.69".

NOTE: (1) A set of old springs can also be used to break-in a camshaft. (2) Be sure and prime the oil system by turning the oil pump over until oil pressure comes up to specs. One way to do this is with a distributor shaft connected to an electric drill. It is then safe to start the engine without scuffing bearings or journals.

You should also check out the timing of your cam to be certain it falls within specifications.

The following illustration shows how this may be done. The cam and timing chain have been installed and a degree wheel put on the crankshaft. A pointer has been affixed above it.

Checking Cam Timing

CLEVELAND V8 RACING HISTORY IN NASCAR & PRO-STOCK

Turn the engine over very carefully (in the direction of normal rotation) until your dial indicator tells you the number one piston reached exact TDC, and set your degree wheel at zero. Place the dial indicator to read the movement of one tappet. (Photo shows special tappet with long bolt affixed). Continue turning the engine over slowly in the direction of rotation, until your dial indicator tells you that your tappet is starting to lift. Stop when you have reached the lift specified for measurement. (Most cams are supplied with a specification card which will tell you the amount of cam lift at which the valve opens and closes. Ford specifications normally call for .100" tappet lift.) Now read your degree wheel. It should agree with the cam specifications within 2 degrees. If for any reason your cam is off more than this . . . or if you wish to run your cam with a different amount of advance or retard . . . you can alter the setting by using D1ZX-6306-BA crankshaft sprocket for 351C engines. This part allows 2 degrees, 4 degrees, and 8 degrees advance or retard (crank degrees). By moving the sprocket one tooth on chain you can achieve up to 28 degrees.

D1ZX-6306-AA . . . for 289-302-351W
D1ZX-6306-BA . . for 351C-400-429-460
D1ZX-6306-CA . for 352-390-406-427-428

Multi-Index Crank Sprocket D1ZX-6306-BA To Advance or Retard Cam

VALVE TRAIN

Intake and Exhaust Valves

The recommended valves are Ford "Competition Only" intakes D0ZX-6507-A and exhausts D0ZX-6505-A. The intake valves weigh 85 grams (compared to 147 grams for stock valves) and are made from solid Titanium with a moly-coated stem. Exhaust valves weigh 95 grams (compared to 123 grams for stock valves) and are made from lightweight stainless steel with a semi-hollow stem and an aluminized face-coating. With their lower mass, they are capable of turning considerably higher rpm (9000 plus) before valve float starts.

CAUTION: Neither of these "Competition Only" valves should be lapped if necessary to true-up seats, because the lapping compound doesn't work well on titanium or the aluminized coating. Instead, true-up value face with a grinding wheel. A conventional wheel can be used on the D0ZX-6505-A exhaust valves, but not on the D0ZX-6507-A Titanium intakes. A Carborundum A-80-04-V10 wheel must be used on Titanium intake valves. These numbers refer to composition, not wheel size. Check with Carborundum for wheel size to fit your grinder.

Valve Spring, Retainer and Keeper

If Ford cam D1ZX-6250-FA cam kit is used, the recommended valve spring is D0ZX-6A511-A. This "Competition Only" three-piece super spring is designed to work with cams that have .600" - .620" valve lift. It produces an installed load of 130 lbs. at an installed height of 1.69". However, it can be used in engines designed for greater spring heights by appropriate shimming. The three-piece spring design consists of strong aircraft quality inner and outer springs and an intermediate damper spring. The inner spring is .100" shorter than the outer spring, which necessitates a .100" "step" in the retainer (preferred) or cylinder head.

The recommended retainer is the stock 351 BOSS piece C9ZZ-6514-A, which has the .100" step. Also use stock 351 BOSS keepers C9ZZ-6518-A and spring seat D00Z-6A536-A.

Three-Piece Valve Spring, Retainer, Keeper and Spring Seat.

To achieve maximum flow and good pressure recovery, the valve face and head seat should be ground according to the following illustrations.

NOTE: The 0.060" wide seat in cylinder head is recommended for ALL types of competition. Do NOT reduce the intake head seat for drag racing, or the Titanium intake valves will wear and distort excessively.

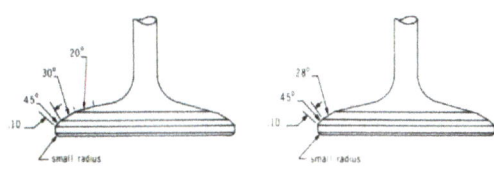

Intake Valve-Seat Face   Exhaust Valve-Seat Face

THE ESSENTIAL SOURCE BOOK

NOTE: Lightweight aluminum retainers are not required or recommended to achieve a stable valve train at 9000+ rpm. However, if you choose to go this route . . . they should only be used for short duration drag strip applications, as the damper spring tends to chafe the aluminum, which requires the oil pan to be checked often for filings.

It is important that valve springs be adjusted to give spring loads which are adequate to control valve float, yet not so high that they cause rapid cam wear. Valve spring heights should be matched to give identical readings and shims added, if necessary, to bring springs up to specifications.

Carefully check the installed spring heights with a machinist's scale or micrometer. Nearly all valve springs are supplied with a set of specifications giving you the proper installed height of the springs. If you use shims to alter the spring height, place them between the spring seat and the cylinder head.

Caution: Never disassemble the inner and outer springs of the D0ZX-6A511-A spring assembly. Since there is an interference fit between the inner and outer coils, it is possible to scratch the surface of the springs and create a potential source of spring failure.

Rocker Arm

The recommended rocker arm set-up consists of stock 351C rocker arms C9ZZ-6564-A and "Competition Only" needle bearing rocker arm kit D0XZ-6A585-A (includes: bearing assy. fulcrum shaft, adjusting nut and set screw). Press the bearings into the outer race. Then slip bearing and race onto fulcrum shaft. They should easily fit into the rocker arms. If there is any interference, the bearings haven't been pressed on far enough and they will wear excessively. When installing the rocker arms, "blue" the valve stem pad of rocker and check for a FULL contact pattern on the valve stem tip, by turning the engine over through a full cam lift cycle. If you do not get a full contact pattern, interchange fulcrum components until a full pattern is achieved on all rocker pads. Torque the Allen head set screw to 15-20 ft.-lbs. This set-up is stable to 9000+ rpm.

NOTE: If the Torrington roller bearings need replacement, they can be ordered under part number B-105 from any Torrington distributor, rather than replacing the whole roller bearing assembly. For very high rpm applications, a number of specialty aftermarket suppliers (Crane, G-K, Iskendarian, etc.) offer aluminum, roller-type rocker arms. If you elect to go for these lightweight pieces, be sure and order 1.73:1 ratio (same as stock 351C).

Set valve lash (intake and exhaust) at .026" - .028" (cold) and .025" (hot).

Stock 351C Rocker Arm With Needle Bearing Kit . . . And Aluminum Roller-Type Rocker Arm (non-Ford part)

Pushrods

The recommended pushrods are stock BOSS 351C items, D0OZ-6565-F. They have a 5/16" diameter, are 8.52" long and are hardened to resist scuffing against the C9ZZ-6A564-A guide plates. As an alternate, larger 3/8" aftermarket (Manley, etc.) pushrods and guide plates can be used if desired for extra durability.

Hardened BOSS 351C Pushrods and Guide Plate

Preparing Cylinder Heads

The recommended cylinder heads are stock 1971 BOSS 351C pieces, D1ZZ-6049-B. They feature polyangle "quench" combustion chambers that are compatible with the engine's "canted" valve train and the TRW No. L-2348-F pop-up pistons. The rocker arm pedestals are machined to take adjustable stud C9ZZ-6A527-A, which is necessary to achieve lash with mechanical cams.

NOTE: The 1970-71 351C-4V engine used similar heads (part number D1AZ-6049-B) except that the rocker arm pedestals were designed to use a positive stop bolt with the stock hydraulic cam. These heads can be used if the pedestals and spring seats are modified as illustrated

CLEVELAND V8 RACING HISTORY IN NASCAR & PRO-STOCK

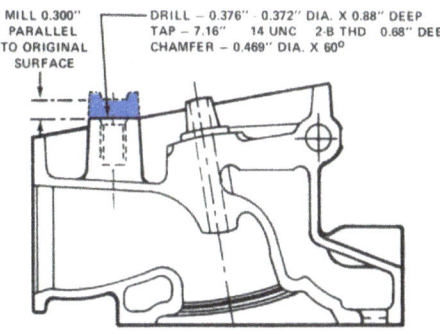

Modifying 351C-4V Heads for Mechanical Cam -- Mill .300" as shown in Fig. above. Be sure and machine parallel to bottom of slot . . . not bottom of head. The slot is at a compound angle to achieve the "canted" valve configuration.

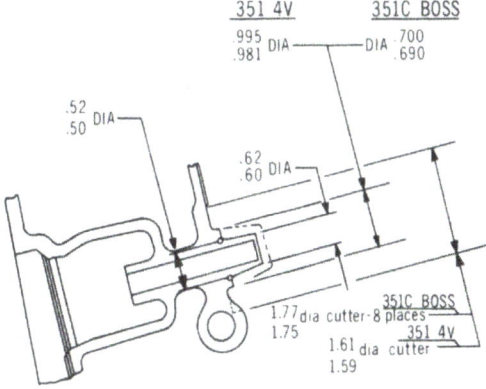

Machine 4V head spring seat to match 351C BOSS.

Once your heads are chosen, the first step in preparing them for competition use is a complete disassembly and cleaning . . . followed by a de-burring treatment, as was done on the block. How far you go with head modifications, of course, depends on the type of competition. For class racing, such as NHRA stock, the only permissible modifications are CC'ing the combustion chambers and a performance-type valve job. Be sure and check the appropriate sanctioning group before starting any work on your cylinder heads.

"High-Port" - Heads

In NHRA Pro Stock and Modified Production drag racing, any head modification is legal. Extensive dyno testing and actual competition has shown that raising the exhaust port adds 20 Bhp @ 8000 rpm, over and above other types of head work. The following illustrations graphically show why this is so . . . note the much straighter route the exhaust gases travel to the headers with "Hi-Port" heads, which of course greatly improves breathing and scavenging. And speaking of headers, a secondary advantage of "Hi-Port" heads is that the exhaust tubing can be more easily routed over the frame side rails of Pro Stock and Modified Production drag machines.

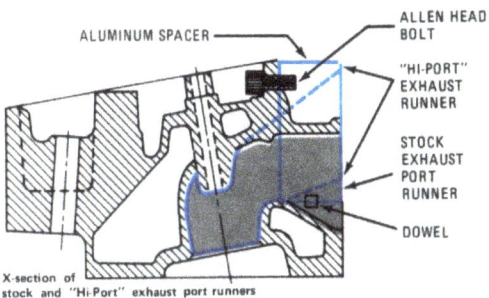

"Hi-Port" Exhaust Runner

"Hi-Port" heads are achieved by machining the head as illustrated, and adding an aluminum spacer plate. It's retained at each end with standard head dowels and four 3/8" Allen-head cap screws, front to rear, as shown.

Cap Screws and Dowels Retain Spacer Plate to Head

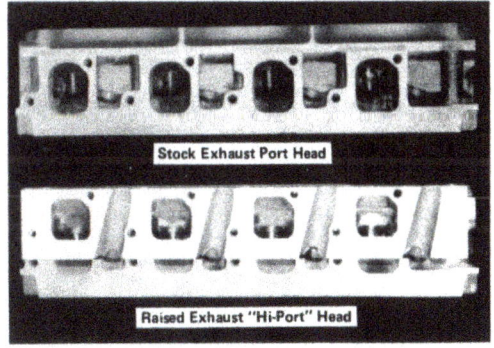

Stock 351C Head/BOSS 351C Head With Spacer Plate

15

"High-Port" Head Availability

"Hi-Port" heads are not available through the Ford Parts Division or Ford Dealers. Hi-Port heads with spacer plate installed, runners ported and polished and combustion chamber polished but face <u>not</u> cut to reduce chamber volume are available from:

Bud Moore Engineering OR	Gapp & Roush
400 North Fairview	32081 Schoolcraft
Spartanburg, South Carolina	Livonia, Michigan
29302	48150
Phone (803) 585-8155	Phone (313) 425-0640

Individual spacer plates are also available for those engine builders who want to do their own thing.

Re-Working Cylinder Heads

> CAUTION . . . Please Read
> Re-working cylinder heads to improve their flow characteristics is highly technical and requires considerable experience and expertise. <u>It should not be attempted by anyone who is not a fully qualified professional in this field.</u> The following specifications and instructions are intended as a guide for high performance machine shops. If you do not fall into this category, contact a competent shop . . . and save yourself a lot of hassle.

Performance Valve Job

The following illustration shows the recommended valve seat face to be machined in the head. The dimensions apply to both intake and exhaust valves; the only difference being the diameter.

CAUTION NOTE: The .060" wide seat is recommended for ALL types of competition. Do not reduce for drag strip use . . . especially if Titanium intake valves are used . . . because they will distort and wear excessively if it's too narrow. Even if other types of valves are used, a .035"-.040" wide seat is not recommended because it doesn't improve flow appreciably . . . and it does reduce sealing area and heat dissipation properties . . . which can shorten valve and seat life. This is especially true if the seat has any runout. Seat and valve life will be much longer if runout is held to a maximum of .001".

Intake and Exhaust Valve Head Seat - This typical progressive-cut performance valve job can be obtained in three cuts as follows: (1) Grind the 45-degree seat, (2) Make a top cut of 30-degrees and (3) Undercut throat at 60-degrees to narrow seat width to .060". Break corner where the throat cut breaks into the port with hand grinder after the valve seat grinding is completed.

The Figure on Page 17 shows a polished, full-race intake port. The valve seat has been cut progressively but with the addition of polishing, the areas above and below the seat have been faired into the cuts, providing the smoothest transition and, therefore, the greatest mixture flow.

A valve job, properly done, will allow you to CC your heads by simply putting a thin coating of petroleum jelly on the valve faces and dropping them in place. See page 18 of this book for approximate thousandths to be removed for each CC milled from BOSS 351C heads. Don't push your luck by milling down to the lowest legal specifications.

Porting and Polishing

Head modifications, other than the progressive seat grinding already mentioned, are usually concerned with porting and polishing. The BOSS 351C head has extremely large ports in stock form. Because of this, mixture flow is very good even without porting or polishing. However, for maximum power output, a fully re-worked head is strongly recommended.

The following figure shows a BOSS 351C head being readied for combustion chamber clean-up. The edges of the chambers have been painted with machinist's bluing and scribe marks drawn, using a head gasket for a template, to form the desired finished shape of the chamber. (Hold the gasket in place with cylinder head dowels.) With the lines for a guide, the two outside edges of the chamber are then ground with a power grinder to fair the edges smoothly into the new contour. This helps to open up the area between the edge of the valves and the chamber wall, improving flow and reducing valve shrouding. Care must be taken to avoid hitting the valve seats with the grinder.

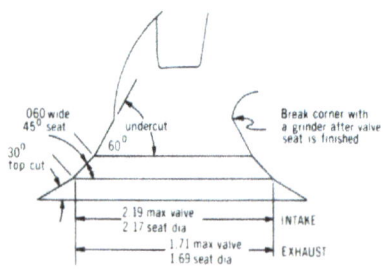

Performance valve job - cylinder head seat.

BOSS 351C Combustion Chamber, Blued and Scribed for Cleanup.

CLEVELAND V8 RACING HISTORY IN NASCAR & PRO-STOCK

The following figure shows the areas of the combustion chamber which are most critical for maximum air flow. The stock BOSS 351C chamber has recessed valve seats which produce a sharp machined edge around the circumference of the seat. Sufficient material should be removed from the areas to fair these edges in, making a smooth transition to the chamber roof.

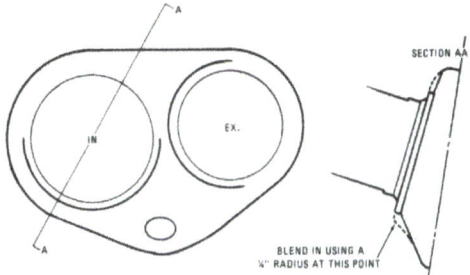

BOSS 351C Combustion Chamber

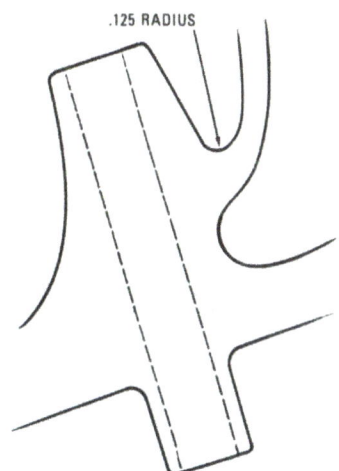

Valve Guide Modification

The next figure shows how the valve pocket should be treated. Stock heads have a partially machined pocket which leaves a sharp edge around the runner throat. Retaining the same diameter as the stock machined cut, the throat should be left straight for the first 1/2" from the seat, before the radius is developed into the curved area. The machined portion should be gradually blended into the "as-cast" pocket, utilizing a generous radius at the point of transition.

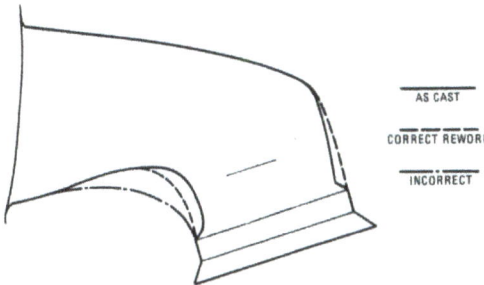

BOSS 351C Intake Port Modification

Valve guides require very little modification. The recommended treatment, shown in the next figure, is to reduce the outside diameter of the guide, equally, by .100". The base of the guide should be blended into the roof of the pocket with a .125" radius and the sharp edge removed from the end of the guide by grinding a small radius.

The intake port runner should be polished to remove any casting irregularities or protusions. Take only the minimum amount of metal required to produce a smooth finish and keep each runner the same dimension and contour to assure equal mixture flow.

Full-Race Intake Port (bottom) and Stock Runner (top).

When intake runners have been completely polished, they look like the above intake ports. All surfaces have been ground to a high polish. Page 15 illustrates the polished exhaust port and spacer plate.

Head clean-up also should include matching the intake ports. This is done by using an intake manifold gasket as a template and then bluing and scribing the surfaces of both the manifold and the head. The ports are then ground out to the scribe marks on both the intake manifold and head.

17

THE ESSENTIAL SOURCE BOOK

Oil Seal Modification - Road Race Only

Another recommended head modification is the installation of Perfect Circle or Raymond type oil seals on the valve stems. These seals provide tighter oil control for full race usage.

NOTE: This type of seal must be installed with three-piece valve spring D0ZX-6A511-A, because the stock 351 BOSS seal will not fit inside the inner spring.

Stock 351C Oil Seal   Perfect Circle Oil Seal

The above figure compares stock oil seals with Perfect Circle seals. Notice that the Perfect Circle seal requires the valve guides to be cut with a special valve guide machining tool, as shown in the figure below, to accept the seals. These tools are readily available from many high performance suppliers.

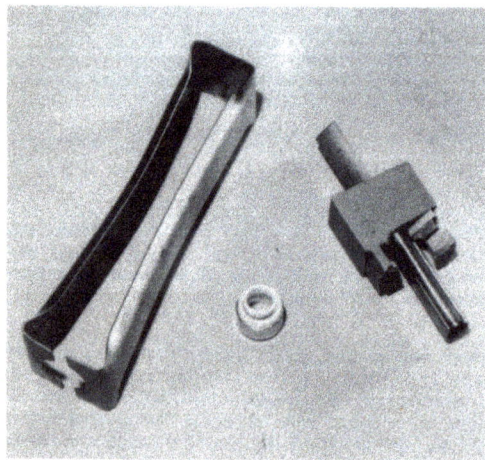

Special Cutter and Installation Tool Required For Perfect Circle and Raymond Oil Seals.

CC'ing Heads

After re-working your heads, it's usually necessary to mill the combustion face to achieve desired legal minimum combustion chamber volume. Stock 1971 BOSS 351C heads have a volume of 64.6-67.6 cc. Polishing the combustion chamber adds about 1-2 cc. The desired volume with the TRW No. L-2348-F pop-up piston and D3ZZ-6051-A head gasket is 61.0-63.0 cc. Milling .006" from the combustion face reduces the volume by 1 cc. Therefore, if we use "nominal" specifications, it means about .033" must be milled off to achieve a 62.0 cc chamber volume.

CAUTION NOTE: In no case should more than .060" be milled from a stock 351C BOSS head. After slabbing heads, check to see that there is a minimum piston-to-valve clearance of .100". Also, do not attempt to use long-reach spark plugs. Always use either a standard, or racing gap spark plug.

Head Gaskets

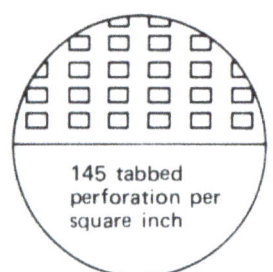

145 tabbed perforation per square inch

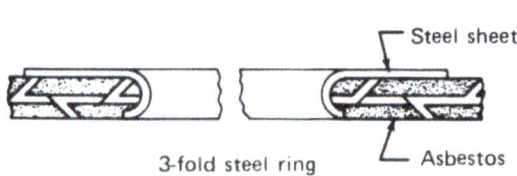

3-fold steel ring around bolt holes

Steel sheet
Asbestos

5-fold steel ring around combustion chambers
Section AA

5-Fold Head Gasket D3ZZ-6051-A

CLEVELAND V8 RACING HISTORY IN NASCAR & PRO-STOCK

The recommended head gasket is a unique OHO 5-fold gasket that's available under part number D3ZZ-6051-A. It feature "U-shaped" steel rings around all bores, together with internal "S-shaped" steel rings that compress to form five super-tight sealing ridges. It was especially designed to withstand high pressures and has proven exceptionally durable in all sorts of competition. It eliminates the need to "O-ring" heads or block to extend reliability.

NOTE: For extended high rpm operation, durability of D3ZZ-6051-A head gasket can be improved by drilling a 5/32" diameter hole as illustrated. This is not required in drag racing, but only where super endurance is necessary. This modification relieves coolant pressure on the gasket to prevent "drumming" and possible early failure.

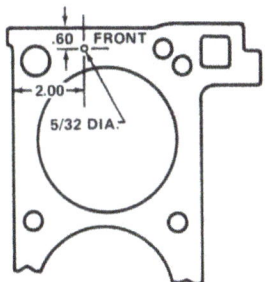

Head Gasket Modification For Endurance Competition -- Not Required For Drag Racing.

Lubrication

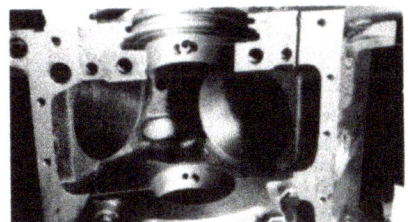

351C Lubrication System

The 351C lubrication system is similar to the 429 engine, in that two main oil galleries, which intersect the R.H. and L.H. lifter bores, supply full pressure to the tappets. The R.H. gallery also supplies oil to the main, con rod and cam journals. The L.H. gallery is connected to the R.H. gallery at a unique three-way junction at the No. 5 main journal. No modification to this lubrication system is required, or recommended, other than using a deep sump oil pan and installing heavy duty OHO 351C oil pump spring D2ZX-6670-AA.

Install oil pump spring D2ZX-6670-AA in stock oil pump.

The stock 351C spring gives a "hot" oil pressure of 35-60 psi @ 2000 rpm, with stock bearing clearances. Heavy duty OHO oil spring D2ZX-6670-AA has 22 coils and 3.03" free length which raises the "hot" oil pressure to a "nominal" figure of 80 psi. It may be a little less (or more-up to 100 psi) depending on engine clearances.

I.D. NOTE: The stock oil pump spring (C5AZ-6670-A) also has a free length of 3.03" and 22 coils. To identify the OHO spring, check either end for two "dead coils" . . . which means coils that bottom out or touch each other.

When installing spring, replace cotter pin with roll pin. This eliminates the possibility of the pin shearing off in competition. A slight improvement in stock flow specs of 13.5 gallons per minute can be achieved by re-working the inlet and outlet ports. However, the increase is minimal and the stock flow is more than adequate for any race condition.

CAUTION: Never, ever, under any circumstance race a competition engine if the oil is not "hot" (ie. water temperature gauge reads at least 160 degrees). This may take considerable warm-up time, but it is most important that oil temperature be about 200-degrees. In addition, 351C Pro-Stock engines must have an oil pressure of at least 50 psi. This should be easily obtainable if the D2ZX-6670-AA spring is installed . . . even if ALL clearances are on the loose side. However, do not exceed recommended clearance specifications. If the oil pressure gauge drops below 50 psi, shut the engine off immediately!

Choosing A Rear Sump Pan

A number of companies offer rear sump oil pan for competition. For Pro-Stock drag racing, a 9-qt. rear sump is recommended, such as offered by Wolverine Chassis or Gapp & Roush. It features a windage tray, trap door, side baffling in sump and comes with full-screen pickup, 3/4" diameter steel-braided line and fitting for oil pump.

THE ESSENTIAL SOURCE BOOK

Oil Filter

Use a high performance oil filter that's compatible with high oil pressure, while maintaining adequate flow . . . such as a WIX "VIP", Fram, Lee or STP.

Tom Smith, Wolverine Chassis, points out "trap door" that allows oil to return to sump, but not escape forward.

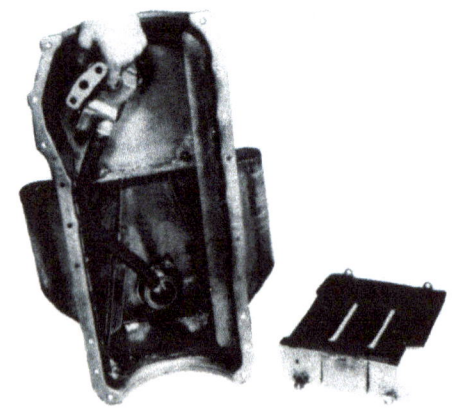

Side bustles in sump are vitally important to assure adequate oil supply to pickup.

The engine compartment photo above shows how to install the filter and achieve necessary clearance by using an ECONOLINE ADAPTER from 240-300 CID engines. These parts are detailed below.

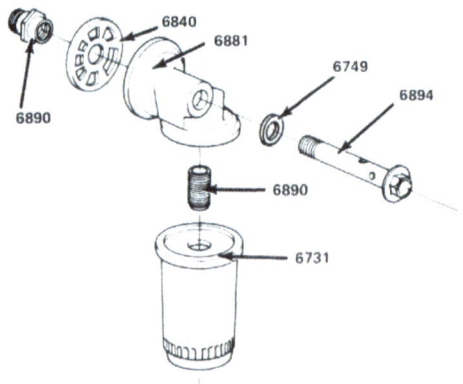

Gapp & Roush pan features doors to allow cleaning of sump. To guard against oil starvation during acceleration, position the oil pickup 1/4" from floor of oil pan with 1/4" thick nuts.

Part Number	Description
C5AZ-6840-A	Gasket-Adapter to Block
EAA-6749-A	Gasket-Head to Hollow Bolt to Adapter
C5TZ-6881-A	Adapter—Oil Filter
B8A-6890-A	Insert-Oil Filter Mounting
EAM-6890-A	Insert-Adapter to Block (3/4"-16 female/ 1 1/16"-12 male 1/2" long)
C5AZ-6894-A	Bolt-Adapter to Block (Hollow) 3/4"-16, 3-17/64" long

CLEVELAND V8 RACING HISTORY IN NASCAR & PRO-STOCK

Carburetor/Intake Manifold/Header Tuning

Induction and exhaust tuning is generally determined by the type of competition. The following recommendations have proven successful in Pro-Stock drag racing, which require high rpm range tuning. For other classes, consult with any of the many performance manufacturers for their advice.

Carburetor

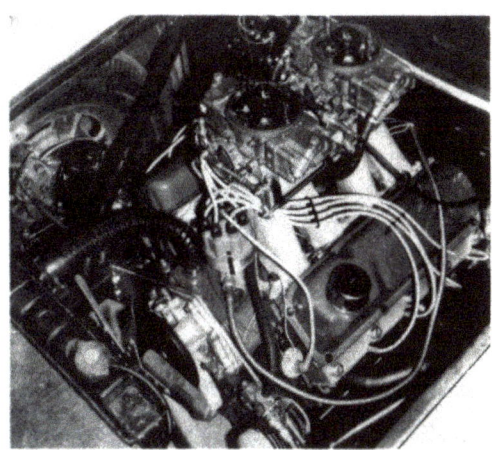

Holley 660 carburetors

A pair of Holley R-4224-AAS carburetors flowing 660 cfm each (total of 1320 cfm) are recommended topside. They feature center accelerator squirter pump, single inlet and side pivot floats.

Carburetor Specifications

Primary venturi diameter	1 1/4''
Secondary venturi diameter	1 5/16''
Primary throttle bore diameter	1 11/16''
Secondary throttle bore diameter	1 11/16''
Air cleaner diameter	5 inches
Primary main jets	No. 76 (22BP-40-76)*
Secondary metering plate	No. 12 (34BP2007-12)*
Needle and seat	.097'' (18BP-213AS)

* These are Holley part numbers for stock carburetor. It may be necessary to change jets to compensate for temperature, altitude or humidity.

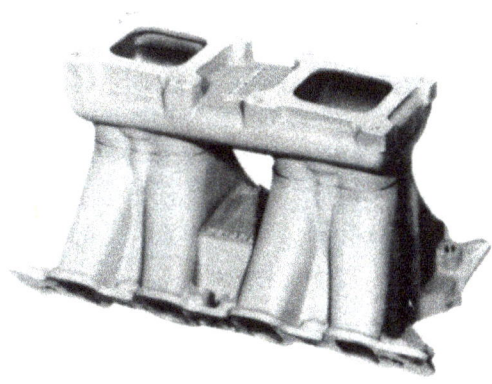

Model No. 1992 Weiand "Tunnel Ram" intake manifold.

A Weiand model number 1992 "tunnel ram" intake manifold is recommended for Pro-Stock machines. It features a top plate that is compatible with the Holley spread flange carburetor, which of course can be replaced for other types of competition. It provides fantastic breathing throughout the power range . . . especially at the top end. The following chart shows the approximate amount to take off manifold when milling heads.

NOTE: If the Weiand manifold is lightened by removing metal from between the runners (see photo at right), then a gasket must be used to cover the "valley" area. The stock 351C BOSS intake manifold gasket (DOAZ-9433-A) is recommended, since it is a one-piece design that includes a center section to cover the valley.

NOTE: If the carburetors are mounted sideways (to allow clearance with windshield), then Holley Fuel Bowl Kit No. 85R-3539 should be installed. This converts the side inlet bowls to dual inlet bowls . . . and more importantly . . . converts the side pivot floats to center pivot floats to prevent closing the fuel inlet during acceleration.

AMOUNT OF STOCK TO REMOVE TO ASSURE CORRECT MATING OF PORTS.

ENGINE (CU.IN.DISP.)	CYLINDER HEAD (INCHES)	INTAKE MANIFOLD Sides (In.)	INTAKE MANIFOLD Bottom (In.)
351C	.010	.010	.014
	.020	.020	.028
	.030	.030	.042
	.040	.040	.057

THE ESSENTIAL SOURCE BOOK

Headers

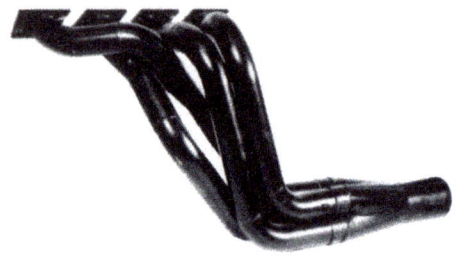

2 1/4" (O.D.) diameter x 34" long headers recommended.

A number of excellent header manufacturers such as Jr. or Hooker can supply pipes for the 351C "Hi Port" heads, since the spacer plates use the same exhaust manifold bolt pattern as stock heads. Just be sure the collector has a 3 1/2 - 4" diameter. The primary pipes should have 2 1/4" O.D. and be 34" long.

Ignition

A dual point, centrifugal advance distributor is necessary for maximum performance at 7000-9000 rpm. Although the '71 351C BOSS and '72 351C H.O. engines came with a dual point distributor, it isn't recommended because it uses a dual advance (centrifugal and vacuum) mechanism. The simplest and least expensive way to achieve a good dual point system that performs well up to 8000 rpm is to install Motorcraft's dual point conversion kit D1AZ-12A132-A. It contains instructions, springs, dual points and plate assembly . . . and can be used in any 351C, 429 or 460 distributor housing, since they all fit 351C engines. For improved performance and durability above 8000 rpm, a high performance distributor such as Accel or Mallory is recommended.

Distributor Calibration with D1AZ-12A132-A Dual Point Kit

Distributor RPM	Distributor Spark Advance
200	0 - 5 degrees
400	0 - 5 degrees
500	0 - .75 degrees
600	0 - 2 degrees
800	2 - 4 degrees
900	4 - 6 degrees
1000	8.5 - 11 degrees (max.)

For Pro-Stock drag racing, total spark advance should be about 43-degrees. Since the distributor curve shown above gives from 17-22 degrees at 2000 rpm crank degrees, it is necessary to set initial engine timing at 26-21 degrees. For most other types of competition, total advance should be 38-40 degrees, which requires initial advance from 23-16 degrees. Adjust the distributor point gap to .018" - .022" (24.5° - 29.0° dwell or 32-35 degrees combined dwell).

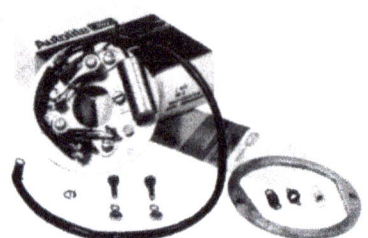

Dual point kit D1AZ-12A132-A

Spark Plugs

351C engine use 14mm spark plugs. The following chart shows Autolite plug numbers for various heat ranges. The AF 501 is recommended for dyno work. Track conditions will dictate selection for racing. CAUTION: Do NOT use "Power Tip" plugs with the pop-up pistons, as there is insufficient clearance.

Heat Range	Thread Size	Standard Gap	Power Tip	Racing Gap
HOT	14MM TAPERED SEAT	—	AF52	—
		—	AF42	—
		AF3	AF32	—
		AF2	AF22	—
COLD		AF1	AF12	—
		AF901	—	—
		AF701	—	AF503
		AF501	—	AF303
		—	—	AF103

COOLING SYSTEM
Radiator

Virtually any small lightweight radiator can be used, as long as it will handle the heat generated during burnouts. Super-lightweight <u>aluminum</u> competition radiators are available from <u>Stewart-Warner</u>. The following chart shows Ford radiators with dimensions similar to the Pinto that can be adapted for Pro Stock applications.

Part Number	Description W	H	T	Fins /inch	Usage
D2FZ-8005-A	17¼	15 1/8 x 1¼			71-73 Pinto 2000
C3DZ-8005-J	17¼	15½	1¼	9	60-64 Falcon 144-170
C3DZ-8005-K	17¼	16½	1¼		63-65 Falcon 260-289, 65-66 Mustang 260-289
C5ZZ-8005-C	17¼	16½	1¼	15	60-65 Falcon 144-170-200, 65-66 Mustang 170-200
C6TZ-8005-P	17¼	17 3/8	1¼		66-73 Bronco 170-200

Water Pump

The stock 351C water pump impeller, with its "straight" blades, causes coolant to begin "cavitation" (formation of partial vacuum) at 5000 rpm; a condition that becomes severe

CLEVELAND V8 RACING HISTORY IN NASCAR & PRO-STOCK

at 6000 rpm. As shown in the chart, this can require excessive horsepower to turn the impeller (especially at 7000-9000 rpm) without significantly increasing flow. Obviously, horsepower used to turn the impeller can't be applied to the rear wheels.

Therefore, the 1970 BOSS 302 impeller D0ZZ-8512-A is recommended for Pro-Stock engines to reduce horsepower losses at 7000-9000 rpm. Cavitation with this "curved" blade impeller doesn't begin until 7000 rpm, and if you cut 1/2" from its diameter, there is no cavitation at 9000+ rpm. Which means you gain about 13 Bhp over the stock impeller.

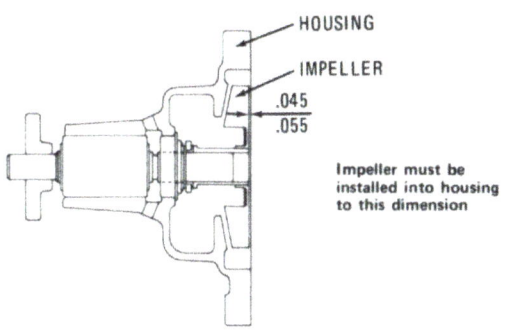

Impeller must be installed into housing to this dimension

D0OZ-8512-A:
Stock 351C-400 Impeller
(straight vanes)

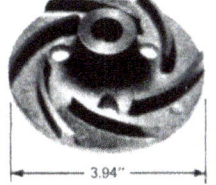

D0ZZ-8512-A:
1970 BOSS 302 Impeller
(curved vanes)

D0ZZ-8512-A:
Impeller with 1/2" cut from diameter
and alternate vanes removed

Water By-Pass Orifice Plate

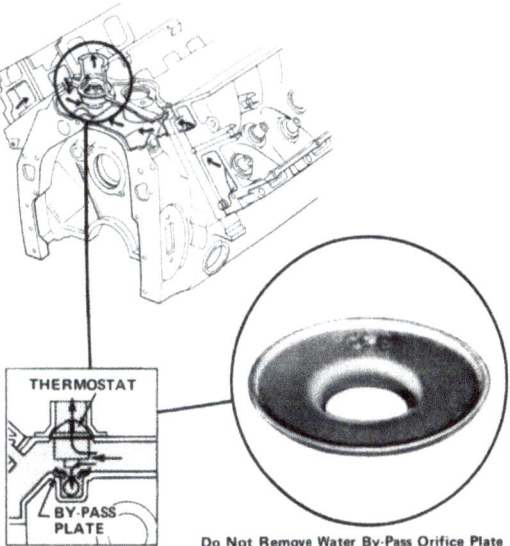

Do Not Remove Water By-Pass Orifice Plate

IMPELLER COMPARISON

Impeller	Engine rpm	Coolant flow gpm*	Horsepower req'd. (loss)
Stock 351C-400 (D0OZ-8512-A)	5000	78.8	5.4
Cavitation begins at 5000 rpm.	7000	85.9	12.4
Becomes severe at 6000 rpm.	9000	82.4	19.7
1970 BOSS 302 (D0ZZ-8512-A)	5000	56.8	2.7
Cavitation begins at 7000 rpm.	7000	79.1	6.5
	9000	84.8	11.7
1970 BOSS 302 impeller (D0ZZ-8512-A) with diameter reduced 1/2"	5000	42.1	1.6
	7000	60.4	3.6
No cavitation at 9000+ rpm.	9000	73.9	6.8

* Gallons Per Minute

In order to modify an impeller, remove the pulley and press the shaft out of the housing, then press the impeller off the shaft. To re-assemble, press the shaft and bearing into the housing. Apply engine oil to seals and install. Then, press the impeller onto the shaft so there is .045" - .055" clearance from the rear face of the housing and end of impeller.

Some racers like to remove the thermostat under certain race conditions. There is nothing particularly unusual about this procedure . . . except with 351C engines. They route coolant water in a unique fashion; directly from the head to the block without passing through the intake manifold.

Coolant water flows from the head to the block, and then into a chamber below the thermostat. When the thermostat is closed, water flows downward through Water By-Pass Orifice Plate (D0AZ-8K517-A), and into the water pump for re-circulation. When the engine warms sufficiently, the thermostat opens and most of the water flows through the thermostat and then to the radiator for cooling . . . with a portion still flowing through the by-pass plate. If the plate is removed, the majority of the water will flow directly back to the water pump, rather than through the radiator . . . thus causing overheating and hot spots.

So the cool tip is to remove the termostat if you like, but do not remove the plate . . . even though it looks like it will restrict water flow. It is designed to do just that.

THE ESSENTIAL SOURCE BOOK

Blueprinting Specifications (Nominal inches, except as shown)

Displacement - Stock Piston 351 CID	
-Trans Am Piston (.020" oversize) 354 CID	
-TRW Piston (.030" oversize) 357 CID	
Bore Stock Piston	4.00
Trans Am Piston	4.02
TRW Piston .030" O/S	4.03
Stroke	3.50
Firing Order (Separate No. 5 & 6 leads)	1-3-7-2-6-5-4-8
Block	
℄ of crank to head face	9.201-9.211
Bore spacing	4.38
Main bearing bore dia.	2.9425-2.9417
Tappet bore dia.	0.8752-0.8767
Cylinder Head	
Combustion Chamber vol.(cc.)	64.6-67.6-stock
	61.0-63.0-slabbed
Valve guide bore dia. (I & E)	0.3433-0.3443
Valve seat width (I & E)	0.060-0.080 -stock
	.060" (performance grind)
Valves-Exhaust	
O.D.	1.7145-1.7045
Stem dia.	0.3418-0.3411
Length	4.94
Valves-Intake	
O.D.	2.195-2.185
Stem dia.	0.3423-0.3416
Length	5.136
Rocker Arm	
Ratio	1.73
Contact pad area with valve foot	80% minimum
Valve Springs—Installed Ht. & Load	
Stock spring	1.82 @ 92 lbs.
3-piece spring D0ZX-6A511-A	1.69 @ 130 lbs.
Piston	
Compression Height-stock piston	1.638-1.624
-TRW piston	1.652-1.638
Deck clearance—(top of piston to top of block)	
Blueprint specs for TRW piston	0.010 nominal
Piston to valve clearance	0.070 min. I & E @ zero leash
Piston Pin	
Diameter	0.9122-0.9125
Length	3.02-3.03
Crankshaft	
Main bearing journal dia.	2.7484-2.7492
Con rod journal dia.	2.3103-2.3111
Connecting Rod	
Length-center to center	5.7785-5.7815
Crank bore dia.	2.4351-2.4369
Piston pin bore dia.	0.9104-0.9112
Con Rod Bearing Crush	.004-.007 per half
SPARK PLUGS	
Type (14 mm. threads)	Autolite AF-701 or 901
	AF-501 Dynamometer
Gap	.025"-.032"

	STOCK	O.H.O. BLUEPRINT
Compression Ratio (nominal)	11.3:1	12.5:1 (with TRW Piston)
Deck Clearance	0.0345-0.0555	0.010
Piston to deck vol.	minus 3.8 cc	minus 8.6 cc (Includes Piston Dome w/Flycut Pockets)
Combustion chamber volume	(Note: Milling 0.006" reduces volume one cc.)	
	66.1 cc	61.0-63.0 cc (slabbed)
Gasket volume	9.85 cc	8.00 cc with D3ZZ-6051-A Head Gasket
Bearings (Select fit mains and rods)		
Main	0.0011-0.0028	0.0025-0.0030 Circle & Road Racing
		0.0035-0.0040 Drag Racing
Rod	0.0008-0.0026	0.0025-0.0030 Circle & Road Racing
		0.0030-0.0035 (Steel) Drag Racing
		0.0040-0.0045 (Aluminum) Drag Racing
Camshaft	0.001-0.003	0.0010-0.0030
End Play		
Crankshaft	0.004-0.010	0.004-0.010
Camshaft	0.001-0.006	0.001-0.006
Con Rod (2 rods) (side clearance)	0.010-0.020	.02-.025 (steel) .035-.040 (aluminum)
Dist. shaft	0.004-0.025	0.004-0.025
Valves		
Valve stem to guide—Exhaust	0.0015-0.0032	0.0011-0.0022
—Intake	0.0010-0.0027	0.0007-0.0018
Valve stem seal to guide		0.015-0.029 Interference
Valve stem seal to valve stem		None (Int. & Exh.)
Valve lash	0.026-0.028 cold	0.026-0.028 cold
	0.025 hot	0.025 hot
Piston		
Piston to valve	0.250	.100 min.
Piston to bore	0.0034-0.0042	0.0055-0.0065
Piston to pin	0.0006-0.0008	0.0006-0.0008
Piston pin to con rod	0.0008-0.0019 Interference	.0010-.0014 Interference (Pressed pin-minimum force of 1800 lbs. to move pin)
Piston ring gap (No. 1 comp.)	0.010-0.020	.014-.016 (drag .018-.020 (circle & road)
(No. 2 comp.)	0.010-0.020	.014-.016 (drag .018-.020 (circle & road)
(oil ring)	0.015-0.069	0.015-0.069
Piston ring to groove (comp.)	0.002-0.004	0.002-0.004
(coil)	snug	snug
Miscellaneous		
Tappet to bore	0.0007-0.0027	0.0007-0.0027
Dist. gear backlash	0.007-0.017	0.007-0.017
Flywheel hub face runout	0.003	0.002
Damper to crankshaft	0.000-0.002 Interference	0.000-0.002 Interference
Oil pump relief spring	50-70 psi	80-100 psi by-pass pressure D2ZX-6670-AA

CLEVELAND V8 RACING HISTORY IN NASCAR & PRO-STOCK

Bolt & Nut Torque Specifications (Ft.-Lbs.)

The following general installation toque specifications apply to operations not listed below.

Thread Size	Torque Ft.-Lbs.
1/4-20	6-10
1/4-28	6-9
1/4-Pipe	12-17
5/16-18	14-20
5/16-24	16-20.5
3/8-16	25-35
3/8-24	30-40
3/8-Pipe	23-28
7/16-14	45-55
7/16-20	50-60
1/2-13	70-80
1/2-20	85-95
1/2-14 Pipe	25-30
9/16-18	110-130
5/8-18	170-190

Cylinder Head – 1st step	60-70
– 2nd step	75-85
– 3rd step	95-105
– 4th step	120
– 5th step	125 (hot torque)
Main Bearing Cap 1/2-13	95-105
3/8-16	35-45
Main Bearing Saddle Width & Cap Fit	Interference
Con Rod Nut (with oil under nut)	55
Oil Pan Bolt 1/4	7-9
5/16	11-13
Cam Thrust Plate to Block Bolt	9-12
Cam Sprocket to Camshaft Bolt	40-45
Flywheel to Crankshaft Bolt	75-85
Crankshaft Damper to Crankshaft Bolt	130-150
Spark Plug (14mm)	10-15
Oil Filter Mtg. to Block Insert	60-100
Carburetor Mtg. Stud	4-7
Carburetor Mtg. Nut	12-15
Clutch to Flywheel	12-20
Intake Manifold Attch. Bolt 3/8-16	28-32
5/16-18	23-25
Front Cover Bolt	12-15
Water Pump to Front Cover Bolt	12-15
Rocker Arm Mtg. Stud	70-75
Distributor Hold Down Bolt	12-15
Exhaust Manifold to Cyl. Head Bolt	15-20
Valve Rocker Arm Cover Mtg. Bolt	3-5

36

Balance and Weight Information
(Grams)

Bobweight (estimated)	No. Required	Stock	TRW
Reciprocating:			
Piston	1	580	510
Compression Ring (upper)	1	18.9	
Compression Ring (lower)	1	18.9	
Oil Ring	1	20.5	
Piston Pin (C9ZZ-6135-A)	1	146.5	
Conn Rod Assy (piston pin end)	1	194	
		978.8	908.8
Centrifugal:			
Conn Rod Assy (crank end)	2	1108	
Conn Rod Bearings	4	87.5	
Oil in Crankpin	4		
		1199.5	1199.5
Total Bobweight		2178.3	2108.3
Less Equivalent External Bobweight of 27.3 oz. in. in Damper and Flywheel		777.1	777.1
Crankshaft Bobweight		1401.2	1331.2

CAM TIMING (@ .100" tappet lift)
Part No. D1ZX-6250-FA

I.O.	18° BTC	Intake Lobe Lift	.355"
I.C.	35° ABC	Intake Lobe duration	326°
E.O.	45° BBC	Exhaust Lobe Lift	.368"
E.C.	13° ATC	Exhaust Lobe Duration	334°

Distributor Calibration
(Using dual point kit D1AZ-12A132-A)

Distributor RPM	Distributor Spark Advance
200	0° – 1/2°
400	0° – 1/2°
500	0° – 3/4°
600	0° – 2°
800	2° – 4°
900	4° – 6°
1000	8-1/2° – 11° Max.
Distributor Point Gap	0.018 – 0.022
Initial Engine Timing	Adjust total spark advance as follows: 38° – 40° - Road & Circle 43° Pro Stock

Conclusion

There were no new V8 passenger car engines made between the introduction of the Cleveland Ford V8, in 1970 and 1991, when the Modular Series was presented, powering Lincoln cars. Only Modular V8 engines were in production, when, in July 2003, Ford issued a statement, estimating that 100,000,000 V8 engines had been made. However, many early V8 engines, including the Lincoln and Ford Y-blocks, and some small-blocks, were omitted from the final count, which suggested this figure was, in fact, reached a little earlier.

Statistics show that, between 1909 and 2002, V8 engines accounted for 53 per cent of the total North American Ford production, with an estimated 39,277,919 V8s manufactured between 1932 and 1966, and a further 66,656,949 between 1963 and 2003. The highest total number of V8 engines produced in a single year was 3,174,200 in 1977, equating to roughly 66,000 per week. During the 1970s, a record 26,029,000 came off the assembly line, and between 1954 and 2000, the Cleveland Engine Plant was responsible for producing slightly less than 25,000,000 V8 engines.

When production of the Cleveland 351ci V8 engine began in July 1969, the predicted demand was substantial. However, by 1973 it had become acknowledged that, because it cost more than the 351ciW, buyers were opting for the latter. Orders for the 351ciW V8 engine far outweighed those for the 351ci Cleveland V8, and questions were raised regarding its viability, which, in turn, led to cessation of production.

A further minor consideration was the substantial costs to be incurred for the necessary re-certification of the engine, in order to make it compliant with the mandatory emission controls in place for the 1975 car model year.

Between 1969 and 1974, an approximate 3,700,000 351ci Cleveland V8 engines were produced in both two- and four-barrel forms (2V and 4V) at the Cleveland Engine Plant Number Two (CEP2) in the USA. The big port quench combustion chamber cylinder heads, fitted in the 351ci-4V engines, made them extremely easy to tune, therefore, in order to achieve high power, modifications were both simple and inexpensive. Production of both the USA-made 351ci-2V and 351ci-4V Cleveland V8 engines ceased at the end of the 1974 car model year, which meant basic manufacture stopped at the end of June that year.

The Windsor Engine Plant Number 2 (WEP2), in Canada, began making 400ci 'tall-deck' block versions of the 351ci Cleveland engine in 1971. Beginning in 1975, WEP2 also produced a 3½in-stroke 351ci version, to become known as the 351ciM. The suffix M, denoting Modified, was added to the title as a means of differentiation from the earlier USA version, which, in comparison, had a low-deck block height. The 400ci and 351ciM engines remained in production at WEP2, with both engines made on the same assembly line, using many common parts, making manufacture of the smaller capacity version relatively inexpensive. When manufacture ceased in 1981, approximately 990,000 of both these engines had been produced.

Although the Cleveland engines have been out of production for many years, adequate amounts of various components are still available, to allow enthusiasts to put good engines together, for either road or racing applications. However, the USA-made 351-4V 'closed chamber' cylinder heads, from the 1970-1971 model year cars, may prove difficult to locate, as, over the years, thousands have been destroyed. However, they can be found,

CONCLUSION

as many scrap yard/breakers yard owners realising the special qualities of these components put them to one side, knowing that potentially they would reap substantial profits. Therefore, for a good sound casting the cost will be high. Engines correctly rebuilt using them will give a good performance.

It is a testament to its design, power output, and reliability, that the Ford Cleveland V8 engine became the choice of top Pro-Stock driver Don Nicholson, and various NASCAR racing teams, including Bud Moore Engineering, Wood Brothers Racing, Junnie Dunlavy, Bill Elliot, and also saloon car racing in Australia. Four decades following its initial introduction in 1970 model year cars, the Ford Cleveland V8 engine remains highly prized amongst Ford car enthusiasts throughout the world.

THE ESSENTIAL SOURCE BOOK

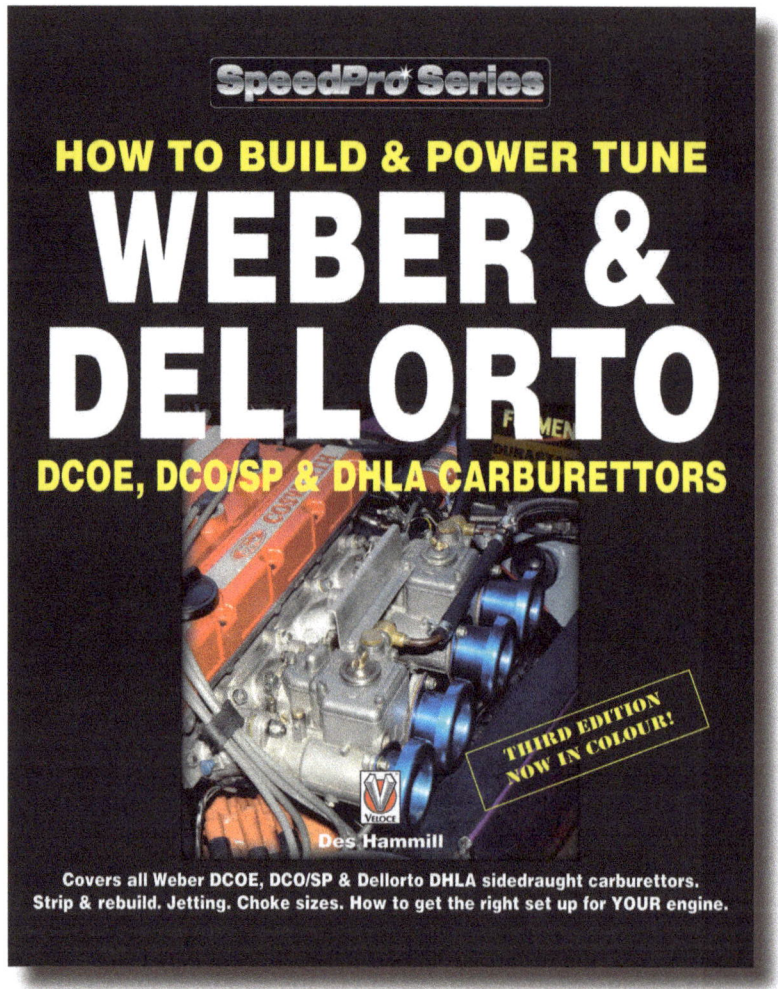

All you could want to know about the most famous and popular high performance sidedraught carbs. Covers strip and rebuild, tuning, choke sizes and much more.

ISBN: 978-1-903706-75-6
Paperback • 25x20.7cm • 128 pages • 181 colour and b&w pictures

For more information and price details, visit our website at
www.veloce.co.uk • email: info@veloce.co.uk
• Tel: +44(0)1305 260068

THE ESSENTIAL SOURCE BOOK

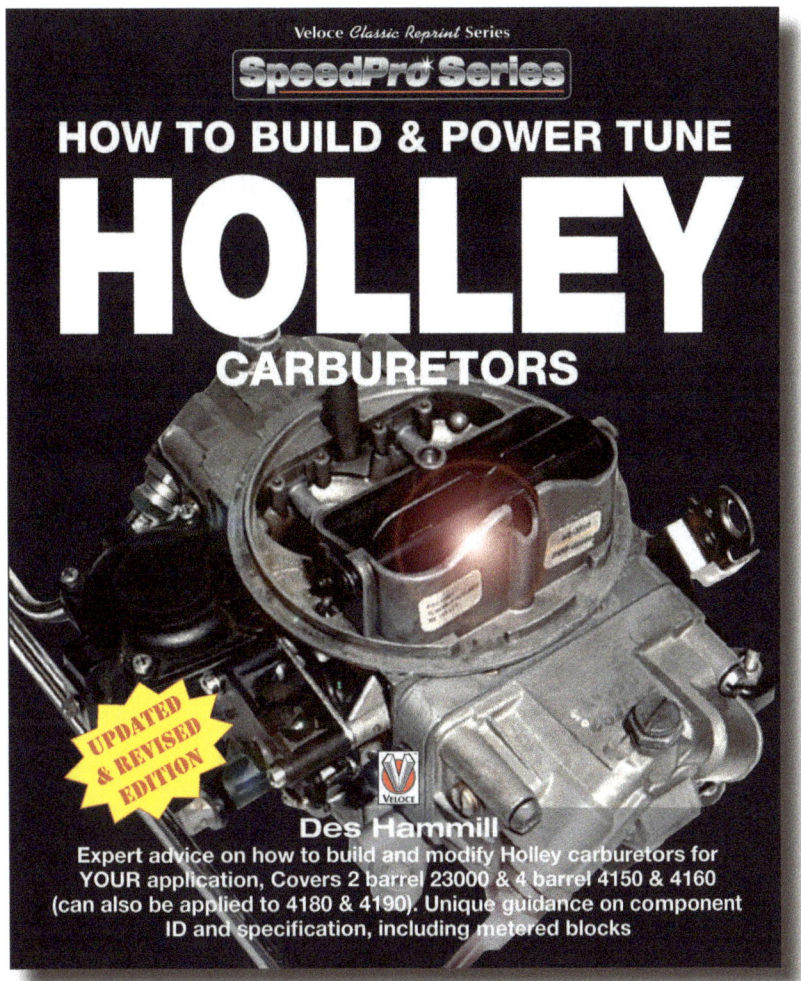

Reprinted after a long absence! The complete guide to choosing and specifying Holley carburetors for engines for road or track performance. This book allows the identification of complete secondhand carburetors and components. Easy to follow tuning instructions to ensure YOUR Holley carburetor delivers maximum performance.

ISBN: 978-1-787110-47-2
Paperback • 128 pages

For more information and price details, visit our website at
www.veloce.co.uk • email: info@veloce.co.uk
• Tel: +44(0)1305 260068

THE ESSENTIAL SOURCE BOOK

There are four crucial aspects of a classic car's performance: straight-line top speed, cornering speed, acceleration, and braking. This book's detailed guidance shows you how to improve each of these, whether for more enjoyable day-to-day use, or for a diverse range of classic motorsport.

ISBN: 978-1-845842-89-5
Paperback • 25x20.7cm • 144 pages • 309 colour and b&w pictures

For more information and price details, visit our website at
www.veloce.co.uk • email: info@veloce.co.uk • Tel: +44(0)1305 260068

THE ESSENTIAL SOURCE BOOK

The process of building 4-stroke engines to a professional standard, from selecting materials and planning work, right through to methods of final assembly and testing, written for the DIY engine builder in an easy-to-understand style, and supported by approximately 200 photographs and original drawings. Containing five engine inspection and build sheets, and the contact details of approximately 45 specialist manufacturers and motorsport suppliers, the book explains build methods common to all 4-stroke engines, rather than specific makes or models. An essential purchase for all engine-building enthusiasts.

ISBN: 978-1-845842-97-0
Paperback • 25x20.7cm • 128 pages • 201 colour and b&w pictures

For more information and price details, visit our website at www.veloce.co.uk • email: info@veloce.co.uk • Tel: +44(0)1305 260068

THE ESSENTIAL SOURCE BOOK

The Essential Buyer's Guides

Having these books in your pocket is just like having a real marque expert by your side. Benefit from the author's years of Mustang ownership, learn how to spot a bad car quickly, and how to assess a promising car like a professional. Get the right car at the right price!

ISBN: 978-1-845847-98-2
Paperback • 19.5x13.9cm
• 64 pages • 108 colour pictures

ISBN: 978-1-845844-47-9
Paperback • 19.5x13.9cm
• 64 pages • 106 colour pictures

For prices and more details, and to see the full range of buyer's guides, visit our website at
www.veloce.co.uk
• email: info@veloce.co.uk
• Tel: +44(0)1305 260068

THE ESSENTIAL SOURCE BOOK

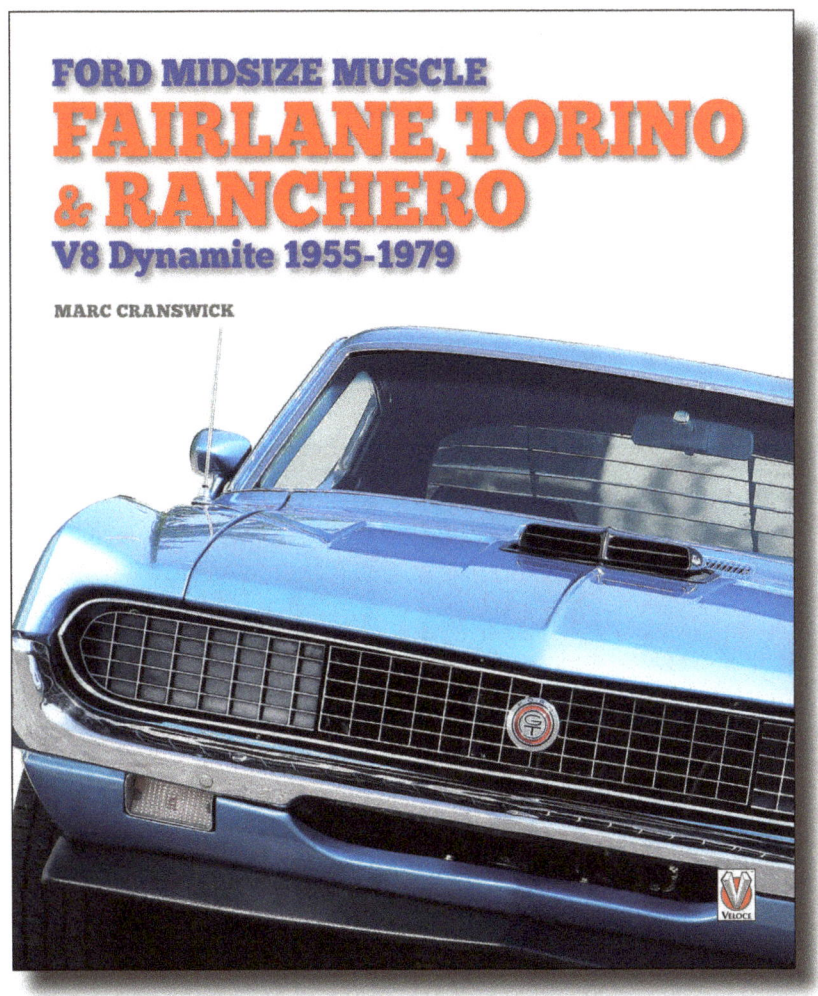

This book details the evolution of Ford's family car through the golden era of Detroit. It tells how Henry took the no-frills Fairlane, added more zing to create the Torino, and satisfied America's luxury desires with the LTD II; and follows the evolution of Ford's midsize muscle cars, to the creation of the first car-based pickup – the Ranchero.

ISBN: 978-1-845849-29-0
Hardback · 25x20.7cm · 176 pages · 229 pictures

For more information and price details, visit our website at www.veloce.co.uk • email: info@veloce.co.uk • Tel: +44(0)1305 260068

Veloce SpeedPro books –

 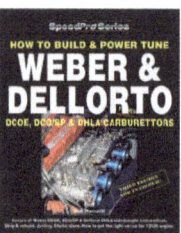    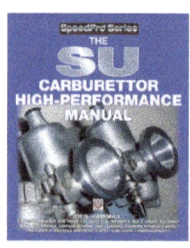

978-1-903706-59-6 978-1-903706-75-6 978-1-903706-76-3 978-1-903706-99-2 978-1-845840-21-1 978-1-845840-73-0

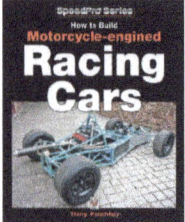     

978-1-845841-23-2 978-1-845841-86-7 978-1-845841-87-4 978-1-845842-07-9 978-1-845842-08-6 978-1-845842-62-8

  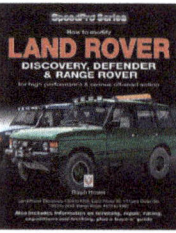   

978-1-845842-89-5 978-1-845842-97-0 978-1-845843-15-1 978-1-845843-55-7 978-1-845844-33-2 978-1-845844-38-7

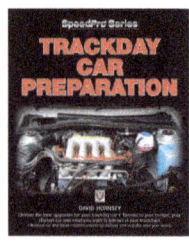 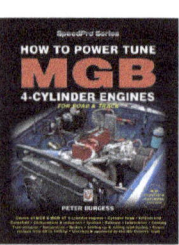   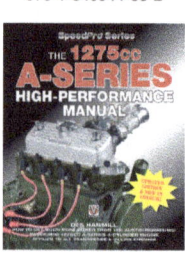 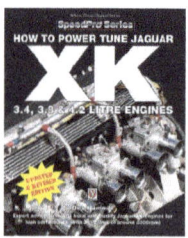

978-1-845844-83-7 978-1-845846-15-2 978-1-845848-33-0 978-1-845848-68-2 978-1-845848-69-9 978-1-845849-60-3

 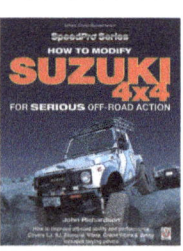 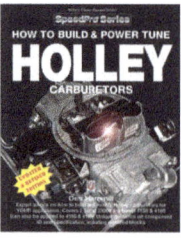 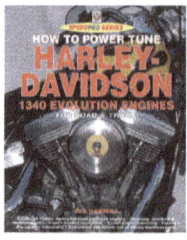 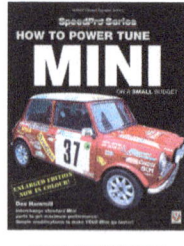 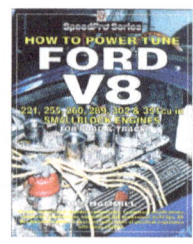

978-1-845840-19-8 978-1-787110-92-2 978-1-787110-47-2 978-1-903706-94-7 978-1-787110-87-8 978-1-787110-90-8

 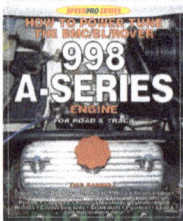   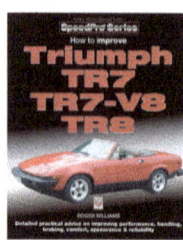 

978-1-787110-01-4 978-1-901295-26-9 978-1-845841-62-1 978-1-787110-91-5 978-1-787110-88-5 978-1-903706-78-7

Index

Acknowledgements 6
Air/fuel ratios 46, 50
Al Martin 8
Alloy cylinder heads – 1982 57
Anti-pump hydraulic lifters 23, 25, 40
ASK 9
Australian built Cleveland engines 13-15
Australian Falcon GTs 13-15
Australian made XE-192540 NASCAR blocks 57, 58
Autothermic pistons 18

Barr, Bill 28
Bedding-in piston rings 35
Benton, Phil 56
Blocking off the piston skirt oiling slots 36
Blocks 17
Blocks fitted with liners 34
Bore wall surface finish 35
Bore wall thickness 34
Boss 302ci Trans-Am 27, 55-57
Boss 366ci engines 53-56
Brown, Paul 49

Camshaft 39
Camshaft durations 39-41
Camshaft lobe and lifter base lubricants for initial start up 40

Car model-year categorisation 9, 10
Carburation and inlet manifolds 43-45
Clayton, Paul 11
Cleveland Casting Plant/CCP 14
Cleveland Engine Plant/CEP 7, 9, 10, 14, 57
Conclusion 86, 87
Connecting rods 18, 26-29
Connecting rod bolts 36
Connecting rod centre to centre distance lengths 27
Connecting rod to stroke ratios 27-29
Coolant temperatures 35
Crankshafts 17, 18
Crankshaft dampers 18
Cuautitlan Engine Plant of Ford Mexico 7, 12

Dearborn Engine Plant 10-12
De Tomaso 12

Emissions 49-52
Engine cooling 46, 47
Engine oil 41
Engine tune-up 48, 49
Engine variants:
  302ci-2V 12, 13, 15-17, 19-23, 27, 39, 41, 44
  351ci-2V 12, 16, 17, 20-23, 25, 26, 28, 36, 39, 41, 44

351ci-4V 12, 16-24, 26, 28, 36, 39, 41, 44
351ciM-2V 16-23, 27, 28 39, 40, 41, 44, 45
358ci NASCAR engines of 1974 and on 56-58
400ci-2V 13, 16, 17, 19-23, 27, 39, 40, 41, 44, 45
Boss 351ci-4V 12, 16-20, 22-26, 39, 41, 44, 49, 56
Cobra Jet/CJ 351ci-4V 12, 16, 20, 22, 23, 39, 41, 44
High Output/HO 351ci-4V 12, 16-18, 20, 22-24, 39, 41
Exhaust ports 21

Farmer, Red 56
Fitting four-bolt main caps onto two-bolt blocks 38
Flat-tappet mechanical camshafts 40
Flywheels 18
Ford Australia 13-15, 57 ,58
Ford catalogue 58-85
Ford draughting definitions 9
Ford management structure 11, 12
Ford North American engine plants 12, 13
Ford South Africa 13
Forged pistons 17
Four-bolt main caps 31-34

INDEX

Fuel 45, 46

Gay, Bill 6, 7, 9, 11
Geelong Engine Plant 12-15, 28, 58
George Stirrat 6, 7, 11
Girolami, Rodney 58
Gordon Ellis 7
Guide plates 25

Head gaskets 54, 56
Horton, Emmet 11

Iacocca, Lee 28
Inlet manifold options 45
Inlet ports 21
Innes, Bill 11
Introduction 6-15
Iskenderian 25, 40

Kar Kraft 54

Lenox, Hank 31
Leonard Wood 56
Lima Engine Plant 11, 12
Low-deck blocks 16, 40

Macura, Joe 7
Martel, Phillip 7
McCord head gaskets 56
McLaughlin, Matthew 54
Moore, Bud 54, 58
Morse, Lee 58

Multi-groove split locks 22
NASCAR 27, 53-58
366ci NASCAR engines 54, 57, 58
Nicholson, Don 54, 55

Oil pump skew gear 38

Parts 49
Pinkerton, Ed 27, 28
Pistons 18
Port and combustion chamber configurations 22
Pre-1970 Ford V8 engine history 10, 11
Preparation for good cooling capability 47
Pro-stock engines 54

Radiators 47
Raviola, Victor 10
Reintz head gaskets 54
Re-ground camshafts 39
Re-using stock connecting rods 35, 36
Rocker arms 23, 24
Rocker arm geometry 23, 24
RX 9

SK 9
SK coded racing engine blocks 53-56
Stevenson, Robert 11
Stock connecting rods in competitive applications 36

Tall deck blocks 16, 40
Tope, Don 57, 58
Torsional vibration 42, 43
TRW pistons 18, 56

Uprating the standard oiling system 29-31

Valve heads sizes 21, 22
Valve lengths 21, 22
Valve lifts 39-41
Valve split locks 22
Valve spring pressures 23
Valvoline oil 41
Venolia pistons 34

Water pumps and alternators 47, 48
Wendland, Robert 55
Windsor Engine Plant/WEP 7, 8, 12, 13, 16, 17

XE 9
XE-192540 NASCAR blocks 57, 58
XH 9
XH coded racing engine parts 54-56

Yunick, Smokey 55

ZDDP oil 41
ZE 9
ZX 9
ZZ 9

WWW.VELOCE.CO.UK / WWW.VELOCEBOOKS.COM
All books in print • New books • Special offers • Newsletter • Forum

www.ingramcontent.com/pod-product-compliance
Lightning Source LLC
Chambersburg PA
CBHW040930240426
43672CB00021B/2995